All Above Board

All Above Board

Creating the Ideal Corporate Board

Ulf Lindgren

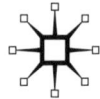

© Ulf Lindgren 2013

Foreword © Michael Treschow

All rights reserved. No reproduction, copy or transmission of this publication may be made without written permission.

No portion of this publication may be reproduced, copied or transmitted save with written permission or in accordance with the provisions of the Copyright, Designs and Patents Act 1988, or under the terms of any licence permitting limited copying issued by the Copyright Licensing Agency, Saffron House, 6–10 Kirby Street, London EC1N 8TS.

Any person who does any unauthorized act in relation to this publication may be liable to criminal prosecution and civil claims for damages.

The author has asserted his right to be identified as the author of this work in accordance with the Copyright, Designs and Patents Act 1988.

First published 2013 by
PALGRAVE MACMILLAN

Palgrave Macmillan in the UK is an imprint of Macmillan Publishers Limited, registered in England, company number 785998, of Houndmills, Basingstoke, Hampshire RG21 6XS.

Palgrave Macmillan in the US is a division of St Martin's Press LLC, 175 Fifth Avenue, New York, NY 10010.

Palgrave Macmillan is the global academic imprint of the above companies and has companies and representatives throughout the world.

Palgrave® and Macmillan® are registered trademarks in the United States, the United Kingdom, Europe and other countries

ISBN: 978–1–137–26425–1

This book is printed on paper suitable for recycling and made from fully managed and sustained forest sources. Logging, pulping and manufacturing processes are expected to conform to the environmental regulations of the country of origin.

A catalogue record for this book is available from the British Library.

A catalog record for this book is available from the Library of Congress.

Ulf Lindgren sadly passed away on 27 June 2012, 57 years old. He was a respected business partner and a loving family father and husband – a true visionary always inspiring his surroundings. He will be remembered for his creative mind and strong enthusiasm towards life.

Always in our hearts,

Wife Ia with children Amanda, Emma, Albert, Greta, Nils, Hugo

Contents

Foreword by Michael Treschow — viii
Acknowledgements — x
About the Author — xiii

1. *All Above Board* — 1
2. The board of the future — 6
3. Enhancing the chairman's value — 18
4. Chairman and CEO: tandem at the top — 29
5. The owner and the board — 40
6. The one team board challenge — 69
7. Leading through times of change and disruption — 85
8. Value creation through innovation: the role of the board — 110
9. Boosting peak performance — 123
10. Setting strategic agendas — 141
11. Summary and conclusions — 156
12. Research methodology — 162

Notes — 168
Index — 169

Foreword

All Above Board by Professor Ulf Lindgren is an interesting and extremely valuable contribution to the discussion on how the work and performance of the board can be further developed beyond control and governance issues. The fiduciary duties of the board member are adding more and more pressure on directors. Liability issues are a reality for many, as is protection from lawsuits and legal pursuits, which are becoming increasingly burdensome.

This is a practical book with focus on how to create a performance culture; benchmarking is not good enough. In addition, public opinion is sometimes hard and often negative in its views about the board. Discussions of bonus schemes to board members are used as arguments not only to curb obvious excesses and greed, but also to effectively make compensation for really valuable services and commitment more and more difficult to entertain.

All combined, these factors make finding and attracting new talent for board membership more and more difficult. At the same time, membership of the board, and especially the Chairman's role, has become more of a profession. It requires significant work and time commitments from a director. In *All Above Board*, Ulf Lindgren discusses how to create a one-team board and the optimal board team, not forgetting individual responsibility.

Another key relationship that must be enhanced and kept in focus is that between the Chairman and the CEO. This is a fundamental success factor for every company.

Also, because of the increasing complexity of organizations, the impact of cycles and disruption, combined with the globalization of businesses and corporations, all put new demands on the competence and skill profile of the board member. Whereas previously, a board membership was the recognition for a long and dedicated career in business and/or politics, a director of today's modern corporation should be recruited using the same systematic and well-defined procedures as when the same companies engage in hiring of new senior management positions.

Ulf Lindgren does not stop with strategy and goal formulation as being key tasks of the board. He is also arguing for a new and more strategic role of the Board: that it focuses on value creation and business decisions, thereby supporting management in strategy implementation and acting as a catalyst for change and innovation. He cites this should be a constant with a focus on how to create a performance culture, by acknowledging that benchmarking is simply not good enough.

In one section of the book, Professor Lindgren brings up the highly relevant issue of the relationship between the owner and the board. He discusses how the board should act to translate the vision and goals of the owner into corporate strategy. He points at the need for a well-functioning interaction between the owner(s) and the board.

This extremely valuable work by Professor Lindgren should be a stimulating basis for extensive discussions in all boardrooms, and shows how to develop its work as a real value creator to the long-term benefit of all stakeholders.

It gives food for thought and reflection – what you can do yourself to improve the performance of a board!

Michael Treschow
Chairman, Unilever

Acknowledgements

The idea to launch the initiative that led to *All Above Board* research came up through challenging discussions with my partner and owner and chairman of the Lorange Institute, Professor Peter Lorange. Peter, who once acted as my mentor when I finished my Ph.D. studies and wrote my doctoral thesis, had asked me to work as the Dean and Executive Director of the Institute he had recently acquired in Zurich. We had both served on the board of directors of both family companies, not-for-profit organizations as well as publicly listed companies. We were also both equally frustrated over the lack of a strategic mindset and value creation focus amongst so many of the boards where we had or continued to serve on. We simply wanted to understand why this was the case and what could be done to enhance the role of the board to be more focused on what we believed should be truly leveraged tasks and responsibilities. We were tired of the waste of time and effort that too often occurred at board meetings and of the political infighting and nonsense discussions.

We questioned why boards did not act as one team but rather as clusters or fractions of groups of interests and egoistic thinking, and we were concerned about the vaguely defined leadership role of the chairman him/herself. Is after all the chairman not the ultimate leader for the corporation?

Therefore, we decided to embark on a project to study how boards and especially chairmen of these boards really acted and thought. In order to conduct this study, we decided to interview and discuss with a prominent group of executives from some of the world's largest and most prestigious corporations to enable us to share their experiences in a systematic way.

Acknowledgements

I am grateful for Peter's wisdom in designing the study and to guide me in the structuring of our thoughts. Although I went on to finalize the interviews without him (we did a dozen or so together), his valuable thinking has been indispensable for the outcome of this work.

I also would like to thank IEDP and its Chief Executive Peter Chadwick who encouraged me to submit the first article for publication in the IEDP journal, *Developing Leaders* (Issue 3: 2011). A huge thank you also to IEDP Executive Editor Roderick Millar, who has contributed fantastic intellectual input to the findings and has been of outstanding value in putting together the final research report from the initiative. Thanks Roddy, without your contribution that work would never have been completed.

It is with thanks to IEDP that the plan to write and publish the book *All Above Board* was conceived. Juhani Anttila of ValCrea in Zug, Chairman of Ascom and board member of several large corporations has also played a key and decisive role in the development of ideas, and has helped me tremendously in the final concluding stages of the book.

I am grateful for the insightful and relevant contribution from Michael Treschow, Chairman of Unilever. Michael Treschow has written the foreword to the book, and was one of the senior chairmen I interviewed at length during my research work. I have also had the privilege of working for Michael Treschow as an advisor during my time with Nordic Management and later with Bain & Company. His profound experience and knowledge about board work and priorities have been extremely helpful in the writing of this book. I fully share his views as expressed in his insightfully written Foreword to *All Above Board*.

I want to extend my deepest thanks to Palgrave Macmillan publishers in London for their keen support during my work. Palgrave has encouraged me to take on the mission to 'spread the word' on the role of the board and the challenges that await board members in corporations worldwide to take their corporations closer to their full potential.

In particular, I want to thank Eleanor Davey-Corrigan and Hannah Fox, who have given valuable input to my manuscript, and helped me to launch this initiative from start to finish.

Thank you to all chairmen and CEOs and senior board members who gave part of your valuable time to meet with me during long hours of engaging in discussions and experience sharing. This report is a merger and summary of your ideas and thoughts on the key issue of what boards should do to create value and improve its contribution to the corporation it is elected to serve.

About the Author

Ulf Lindgren founded the Nordic Management Group in Scandinavia in the 1980s. The company was sold to LEK Consulting in 1990, where he became a Senior Partner and Principal.

Ulf has since been a Director and Board member of Bain & Company International Inc. and Founder and Managing Partner, Bain & Company Nordic. He was actively involved in the foundation of Bain Capital Europe in the late 1990s. He remained a senior advisor to several private equity firms.

He was Co-Founder and Executive Chairman of Net Insight AB (Nasdaq/OMX). He was also Co-Founder and Executive Director of BTS Group (Nasdaq/OMX). He was an investor and board member of Graphco Technologies Holding Inc. in the United States. (OTCBB), Realviz SA (sold to Autodesk) in France, NetGameFactory AB (sold to Essnet Group) in Sweden and Focus Media Group SA (sold to AT&T) in Switzerland and the United States.

Ulf Lindgren was an investor and Executive Director of Videosoft Security Systems Pte Ltd, Singapore, of Spintel AB, Sweden and Safe Technologies Limited in the UK.

He served as Senior Advisor and board member of several large global corporations through his London based advisory company, Nordic Advisors Limited. He was involved in the establishment of Endeavor Inc., U.S.A. (a not-for-profit organization), and served on Endeavor Global Advisory Board from the start until 2005. Most recently, he was a director and principal investor in Safe Technologies Limited, United Kingdom.

About the Author

Ulf Lindgren has a Master of Science in Management and Business from the Stockholm School of Economics (1976) and a degree in Russian Language and East European Studies from the University of Uppsala (1977), as well a Master of Law (Jur kand) degree from the University of Stockholm (1978).

He has a Ph.D. degree in International Mergers and Acquisitions from the Stockholm School of Economics (1982), which included participating in the Individual Studies Programs at Harvard Business School 1980–81.

Ulf Lindgren was also Assistant Professor of International Business and Finance at the Stockholm School of Economics, and has been a Visiting Lecturer at IMD (CEI) and IFL (Swedish Institute of Management). He has been Adjunct Professor of Entrepreneurship at INSEAD, and was most recently Visiting Professor of Entrepreneurship at the Stockholm School of Entrepreneurship. Lindgren was also the Dean and Executive Director of Lorange Institute of Business in Zurich.

Ulf Lindgren spoke fluent Scandinavian, English, French, and Italian and had a good working knowledge of German, Spanish and Russian. He had been a player in the Swedish Second Division in football (soccer) and in the First Division in squash. Ulf was the skipper/owner of a 36-foot sailing yacht with three second place positions in the Open IOR III class in the Around Gotland Offshore Race.

He was married and had six children.

Chapter 1
All Above Board

The board is a vital part of all corporations and it is the ultimate leader of the organization. The board has been appointed and represents the owner as well as the shareholders. It has been assigned a key role in all forms of corporate governance as defined by law, codes of conduct, and by practice in all countries around the world.

Strong leadership should be exhibited by the board and is imperative for success. Many times, we look at the CEOs and their management teams when discussing leadership of a company.

However, we know that the board is another layer of decision making and governance that impacts the strategy and structure of the business. The board sets long-term strategic direction for the business. It allocates the key resources to the core, formulates strategy, and is responsible for implementing corporate governance. It appoints and removes the Chief Executive Officer.

The Chairman is leader of the board. He/she is the ultimate leader of the corporation. As such, I am of the firm belief that the role and leadership of the board could be enhanced to become even more focused on value creation. The board should lead the company to reach its full potential. This is the key role of the board.

This book is about how the board and its members could better define its role and focus its tasks and modus operandi to achieve its core goal.

The book deals with how boards work or do not work in large corporations around the world. It also shows how excellent corporations have defined the role and work processes for their boards.

I have had the opportunity to meet and discuss with some of the heads of industry in some of the world's leading corporations. I have shared their experiences and developed new ideas and themes for how we could improve and enhance corporate governance and the role of the board. In this book, I have aimed at summarizing the essence of such experience sharing discussions. Hopefully, these experiences could work as input for other corporations when designing and implementing the framework for launching a new and value-focused board.

If this is possible, my work has been worthwhile.

And above all, All Above Board!

Reality case

All Above Board: Steve Jobs and the change at Apple

This is the story of the change process at Apple as it has been told to me, because I did not have a chance to meet Steve Jobs during my research, although I would have loved to do so. I did have the privilege of meeting Steve Jobs on a previous occasion when discussing a possible sale of one of my portfolio companies to Apple.

I am still impressed by his vision and insights that we discussed during our meeting. With his premature death, the world has lost a great businessman, visionary person and leader. But let us study the way he used Apple's board at the time of his return to the company in 1997. The following events and story are based on studies of other sources, especially from the book *Steve Jobs* by Walter Isacsson (Isacsson, 2011).

As we all know, Steve Jobs was more or less forced out of Apple by a group of executives and board members under the leadership of Gil Amelio, who eventually became the CEO of the company. Apple went through very hard times and Jobs was asked by the board to come back to rejoin Apple in 1997. In the beginning, he was not asked to become the new CEO to replace the outgoing (replaced by the board) Gil Amelio. Instead, Jobs took on the role of an advisor. However, with the goal of rejuvenating Apple and getting it back from the brink of collapse, Steve Jobs needed to secure full degrees of freedom to act without the restrictions of a board that might not have fully supported him.

Thus, before even starting out on his task as the new advisor to Apple, Steve Jobs understood that he needed to completely change the board. Not just a few individuals, but in fact the entire board with the exception of just one board member by the name of Ed Woolard. It was Woolard who had taken the initiative to persuade Steve Jobs to return to Apple and possibly save the company from a total disaster. He was to engage as an advisor and also as a board member. The latter position was to become an imperative to initiate and control the forthcoming reorganization of the Apple board.

Woolard's first request was that the board should fire Gil Amelio, the CEO. It has been said that Steve Jobs was the mastermind behind this decision, even if it was left to Woolard to be the 'Messenger Man' who delivered the news to Amelio.

Once he had come onboard, Steve Jobs became more and more involved in the strategic management of Apple. But his priorities remained with getting two cornerstones of governance in place; first, he secured the loyalty and commitment of the senior management team by restructuring the old and worthless stock option program through a repricing of the strike price of the options. (This was legally possible at the time). Having been reluctant to approve of this controversial action, the board eventually approved of the new scheme.

The immediate next step from Steve Jobs was to request a total restructuring of the entire Apple board. In fact, Jobs made it clear to Woolard, that unless all board members with the exception of Woolard himself immediately resigned, he himself would leave Apple again. The board members reluctantly agreed to leave, but requested that Gareth Ghang, one director stay behind.

In July of 1997, the board formally resigned, just one month after the initial request of Steve Jobs for the complete overhaul of the existing board. This also marked the time for bringing new board members on as directors. One of these new board members was Larry Ellison of Oracle. Others were Bill Campbell, former Apple marketing manager and at the time CEO of Intuit and Jerry York, CFO of IBM. He also met and discussed but never engaged a significant number of potential candidates.

Over the coming years, Steve Jobs would bring on some very prominent and respected people to the Apple board, such as Eric Schmidt from Google, Genetech's Art levinson and Al Gore. But the initial moves when coming back to Apple proved to be decisive for his ability to implement the fundamental change program that Steve Jobs had in mind for the business.

Having reorganized the corporate governance and management structures, Jobs could then go on to take Apple through one of the most fundamental and successful change processes that any corporation has ever undergone. A change program that has seen the events of the launch of the iPhone, the iPad, iPod, the new Mac Notebook series and other product success stories.

From when Amelio was asked to leave in July and until Steve Jobs took control in August 1997, the stock price doubled. This was to mark the beginning of a value creation process that the capital markets have rarely seen before. Today the Apple stock price is close to $600 per share, that is, it has increased by a factor of over fifty times since Steve Jobs started his change program by designing a new board and governance structure.

The lessons to be learned from the story of Steve Jobs' return to Apple are many. For the purpose of this book, however, we stay with the issues related to how he used corporate governance and the board as the key platforms for the launch of his forthcoming change program.

He realized that not only did he have to get rid of the existing board members, after the forced departure of the CEO, but he also needed to build a new board with the right composition of skills and backgrounds to support him and management in building in what was to become one of the most successful companies ever seen.

Lessons to be learned

Reality Case: 'Steve Jobs & Apple'

- A major change program requires a full commitment from and support by the board.
- The composition of the board must be designed to meet the specific requirements for and needs of the corporation at a given point in time, not at least in times of major change.
- A CEO must have been given the full mandate from the board before launching a major restructuring and change program.

Chapter 2
The board of the future

The board of directors: the 'hidden asset'

Should the boards of Lehman Brothers, Bear Stearns, General Motors, Northern Rock, Saab Automobile, Beyond Petroleum and others have been able to avoid the disasters that subsequently hit these corporations? Could their boards have been much more proactive at an earlier stage so as to lead the companies into different and more sustainable strategic avenues and business models?

Although it is obvious that the boards alone cannot be blamed for these crises, we can debate whether they should have been able to guide the corporations into strategic actions and paths to prevent it from occurring in the first place.

In many corporations, the Board of Directors are simply not performing to their full potential. Observing the corporate board composition of most large companies around the world, it is clear that they consist of very prominent and experienced members, often with vast personal contact networks, management experience, customer inroads and indisputable skill sets. Why is it that this 'Hidden Asset' is not used to deliver the results it surely has the potential for?

Are shareholders not paying enough attention to the performance of the board? Or are there built-in flaws in the internal procedures of the board itself that keep it from performing to its full potential? Perhaps the boards simply focus on the

The board of the future

wrong things, too much on regulatory and legal issues, financial reporting and compliance issues versus too little focus on strategy and value creation, and challenging the CEO and his/her top team's strategy and goals.

One team

In the ideal world, if we were free to design and find the optimal Board Team, we would look to a set of imperatives when making the selections:

- Boards would appoint members who complement each other, bring key skills and expertise to the board and enhance quality and accuracy of decision making. Cultural and gender diversity should also be part of the profile definition.
- Boards must make everyone understand that they all serve the interest of the Company; they are not selected to look after self and factional interests, and they must be committed to giving the CEO and his team their full support.
- Boards must avoid involving members who cannot listen and/or who like to listen only to themselves. How many times are boards forced to sit in and listen to the 'Monologue of Director X' who can go on forever until another director or the chairman forces him/her to stop?
- Boards must avoid drawing on the 'Old Boys Network'. This network, when it exists, is often biased towards one industry, gender, geography, and so on. The board must stay clear from the 'club atmosphere' and develop high standards of professionalism and effectiveness. It also should stay free from 'I'll scratch your back if you scratch mine' syndromes.
- The relationship between the CEO and the chairman is a key imperative for all boards to promote; without a well-functioning chairman to CEO interaction, the board's work is doomed to fail. Bearing in mind that the CEO reports to the chairman, as well as the fact that the ultimate responsibility of the board and thus its chairman, is to hire

and fire the CEO, this requires that the roles and tasks of these two 'captains' must be clearly defined and executed upon.
- Chairman and CEO should never be the same person. They must be assigned to two people with complementary skills and profiles, and with a personal chemistry that benefits their relationship. Finally, it is ultimately the task of the chairman to promote the 'One Team' spirit and modus operandi. By setting the standards and following up on individual board member performance, he/she can actively promote and build a board consisting of team players who set the Company's interests first and their own aspirations and objectives later.

Agenda and strategy

Far too often, board meetings are spent on issues far removed from what is of strategic importance to the Company. Meetings become filled up by operational items and with legal and compliance issues, and so on. Sometimes a whole board meeting can be devoted to presentations by many (sometimes all) of the top executives of the firm. These 'Powerpoint Waterfalls' can prove to be destructive for strategic decision making. Too many times the agenda is drawn up in haste without any strategic focus in mind. How many times are the same agenda items from the last meetings just copied over to be used for the next one?

Many formal issues can be circulated and subsequently dealt with beforehand, such as legal and financial reporting issues. Here the board must require more proactive work from the CFO and the Chief Legal Officer respectively.

The chairman seems to have the task to put together an agenda with a strategic focus, perhaps assisted by the President/CEO. However, it is important to stress that the chairman must not 'abdicate' the task of driving the agenda-setting process. The agenda determines the content and the quality of the board meeting, and thus is imperative for the entire functionality of the board. This is a factor that is often overlooked and forgotten. The chairman must be prepared to say 'no' to requests for putting various non-strategic and legal issues on the agenda. This enables the board to stay focused on strategic decision making and not turn the meeting into a 'discussion club' lacking focus and without deliverables.

The committees

Many boards today operate a set of board sub-committees such as the Nominating Committee, the Compensation Committee, the Risk Committee, and sometimes even a Chairman's Committee.

When structured and defined in the right way, committee work can be of great help for the chairman to leverage time to stay focused at the main board meetings. Committees can be both helpful and enhance the effectiveness of the board, including contributing to significantly better decisions. But committees can easily become isolated 'silos' giving themselves specific, and non-strategic, narrow mandates. The risk of creating unnecessary filters and bureaucracy cannot be over-stressed. Instead of freeing up and leveraging the time for effective board work, committees can seriously add to sclerosis and prohibit action-oriented execution of board decisions, which must be avoided at all cost.

Our research indicates that in some cases, the Chairman's Committee had become the real board, that is, where the real strategic decisions were being made. This can be a faster route to decision making, but it is risky, as it reduces the significance of the main board itself. The role and mandate of each committee must be made clear to everyone, and at all costs they must be stopped from becoming 'silos'.

We recommend that the chairman meets with each such sub-committee beforehand and that he/she gives a summary of the key recommendations to the board; not the sub-committee itself who could be expected to sometimes lose proper context.

Overall, given that committees must be put in place as required by the law, they should be used intelligently. However, if we were to have our way, we would rather not have them at all.

Board and innovations

Innovation is essential to the firm's long-term success. Regardless of industry and business situation, businesses must constantly strive for innovations and new ideas to develop key products and services to target customer groups. Innovations allow us to charge higher prices.

Innovations lead to growth and create the market by driving demand for new solutions. The board is essential to pushing for innovation. Often, the board satisfies itself that a certain amount is spent on Research & Development (R&D) and perhaps that a certain part of total revenue comes from new products. However, a healthy strategy calls for more.

The board must ask and push for examples, and constantly discuss with the management team how the key products are being 'innovated on' to satisfy the target customer group's requirements. These are the issues that should be on the board's agenda. The discussion should not be on general long-term R&D, but rather on what is really 'new'. How well are we meeting key customer's demands for new solutions and services?

This requires a thorough understanding of customer needs and a willingness by board members to learn more about key customers and their requirements, as well as their willingness to spend more on truly unique solutions. Successful board members tend to grasp the underlying customer economics, that is, how the solutions that the company is offering impact on the economics of the customer's business model. How many times does the CEO bring board members to key customer meetings? Such initiatives should be part of every board member's learning process when he/she joins the board of the company.

Challenge the paradigm

A vital imperative for the board must be to challenge the way the company conducts its business, how value is being created, and how resources are being deployed. Are we really doing the right things? And, are they being done in the right way?

The board must be prepared and willing to 'think big', to stretch the business beyond its traditional boundaries in terms of business model, performance goals, and so on.

Most companies live under some form of reigning 'paradigm', the mantra through which its business is carried out. The best leaders tend to challenge such accepted 'truths' and continue to push for new and breakthrough initiatives. This is what we believe a board should be doing: to constantly challenge the paradigm, to stretch the limits and to strive for excellence in every aspect of the company's business.

This could imply developing new and disruptive business models, either from within the existing strategic scope of the company or let it emerge as a separate business model in a dual structure. Few boards seem to have the courage and conviction necessary to engage in such bold strategic moves.

We have seen examples where the chairman is pushing his fellow directors to approach the boundaries of the business, to stimulate and encourage management to 'think-out-of-the-box', and have achieved astonishingly good results. But it has been based on a high degree of mutual respect and exchange of views; typically, the board has been turned into a true 'meeting place' where ideas and views are being openly presented and debated, the challenger of the *status quo* is not being branded a 'villain' by his/her peers, but rather is shown respect and an open-minded reception of such suggestions for new and ground-breaking thinking. This is what we have seen happen at some truly world class boards, under the strong and visionary leadership of a non-conformist chairman.

At the same time, many existing corporations are being challenged by new entrants adopting new and disruptive technologies, and sometimes entire new business models. We see this happening in financial services, airlines, retail, and other sectors. Again, the board must act as a catalyst for new thinking and constantly challenge its CEO and his/her team to be watching out for these 'new kids on the block'. There are too many examples of how strong companies have been brought down because of lack of insight about new trends and ideas; how they miss out on being a 'learning organization' and live on based on their past successes. Here the chairman has a great responsibility to foster a never-ending search for strategic excellence.

Pursuing the performance-based culture: creating the 'gap'

There is a clear pattern that many boards tend to be satisfied with the existing way things are being done, as long as the performance of the business is in line with what other comparable businesses are doing. Yet, truly successful companies go beyond that and their boards tend to be asking for even more all the time. They are never satisfied to be 'as good as the best'. As one chairman put it to us: 'Benchmarking is for losers. The winners are those who create the Gap.'

This form of active and demanding leader is what makes the difference between winners and losers, those who create the 'Gap' and those who are satisfied in trying to fill it. But it is not enough to never be satisfied and push for more; the board must be so well prepared that when it asks management to go back and improve their results and plans, it must understand more about why and how this could be done than sometimes even the management itself. This requires reliable and fast information along with its interpretation. This is the level of excellence that a board should strive for in a world-class corporation today.

Only then will the constant challenging of the results presented by the CEO and his/her team lead to changes in behaviour and create world-class results. Such mutual respect exists in some of the successful boards we have observed creating superior results for the business that they are serving.

This successful relationship starts with the chairman and his directors. They must themselves be high performers and deliver superior results in support of the CEO and his/her Team. When this happens, we have seen how the entire organization develops a culture of performance orientation. Values are aligned between the executive team and the board. Such a performance-based culture tends to remain with the organization even if the board is being changed. In effect, these corporations have shown a constantly superior performance.

The culture of such 'Gap'-creating organizations is characterized by focus on speed, action and results. Fast actions are being rewarded and become a natural element in the values adopted by these successful companies.

Such 'Quantum Leaps' distinguish world-class companies from the rest and the winners from the losers. This can almost always be traced back to the board and its strong leadership. The next generation boards must focus on how to work better, by adopting a customer focus and by daring to challenge the eternal truths, the 'sacred cows' of the corporation it serves.

Ultimately, implementing this is the task of the senior executive management, but the board's role is to push for this.

Reality case

A day in the boardroom[1]

The CEO and the Chairman are both sitting in the large conference room dedicated for the Group board meetings. They are putting together the last-minute reports to be attached to the board agenda document. They are also considering what to put under the agenda point 'Other Items'.

The deputy chairman enters the board room. He has been asked to present his suggestions for such 'Other Item' issues to be discussed at the very end of the meeting. Not because they were not considered important, but simply because the 'Other Item' point was always put at the end of the agenda and thus dealt with last. The CEO then tells the chairmen that he asked two of the major business area executives, who were not board members, to prepare a brief on the state of the business in each of them and present any important points for discussion to the board.

Now, the chairman and CEO argue that there would not be enough time to deal with all of them at today's meeting. Thus, the deputy chairman agrees to bring his suggestions back and present them at the next board meeting three months later. The deputy chairman is quite disappointed about this outcome, but accepts the decision. Obviously something important was about to be discussed, perhaps even decided, that related to the core business areas.

The board meeting is scheduled to start at 9 AM.

One by one, the other board members arrive. One board member has been travelling the entire night from the US West Coast, whereas one came in from another board meeting that he had attended in Mumbai. Both seem tired and show signs of jet lag.

Finally, all twelve board members arrive, including the two union representatives. None of the directors is a woman. The board of this large industrial group, one of the largest companies in Scandinavia, has allocated three hours for the meeting. Time is important so the agenda must be followed very strictly.

The chairman opens the meeting and goes on to the first item, 'Minutes from the Last Meeting'. Forty-five minutes later, this item is finally put to the minutes and the chairman goes on to Agenda Item number two; 'Results for the 2nd Quarter 2011'. Here the CFO enters and starts handling the remote control for his long presentation, including eighteen slides.

He goes through the quarterly results and asks the board to approve the results as they were presented. The CFO had sent out the financial results to the board members the previous day so they could have a chance to review the data. However, as most of them had been travelling to come to the meetings, this was not the case for all of them. As a result, the financial presentation and discussion takes almost forty-five minutes as well.

The next item on the agenda is to approve a set of legal documents. These are presented by the Group Legal Officer. They relate to two foreign acquisitions where share purchase agreements have been signed subject to board approval. As with the financial reports, the legal department has sent the signed agreements to each board member ahead of the meeting. Nevertheless, the Group Legal Officer has to ask each board member for questions and comments.

One board member, who previously had been critical to the proposed growth initiative for this specific business area, is occupied by the guarantees that were included in the acquisition agreements. He insists on a review of the warranties by another legal expert, as he views them as too weak for the purchaser, that is, this group. After a discussion, this request is rejected by the rest of the board. The agreements are approved.

Now the Chairman suggests a five minute break. By the time the board reconvenes, it is already 11:05 AM.

After the break, the CEO presents the head of the second largest business area of the group. He tells the board that they have prepared an overview of the strategic situation of the business. The business area head starts on what turns out to be a thirty minute presentation of his division. As this is the segment where one of the two acquisitions has been made, the board member who had previously expressed his concerns and objection to prioritizing this specific part of the group's business again raises his voice.

'I want this board to approve to appoint a strategy consultant to carefully review this business area', he explains. 'I have discussed with one of the world's leading consulting companies, and they have agreed to submit a proposal to the board for a strategy review that they could start right before the summer holidays'.

As everyone on the board was aware of this particular board member's critical view regarding this business segment, they are not surprised, but still the Chairman did not expect that such a request would come up. Therefore, he is not prepared for such a proposal from this board member.

As the discussion of the proposed strategy review lasts for almost a quarter of an hour, the Chairman has to take the matter to a vote. Time is running out and the end of the meeting quickly approaches. The result of the vote is a clear 'no' to the proposed study. The only director in favour of the motion is the board member proposing the study himself.

With only ten minutes left of the meeting, the Chairman now moves on to the last agenda item, 'Other Items'. Just one such item remains on the agenda as the two additional items prepared by the deputy chairman have already been removed from today's meeting.

Before the meeting went on to the Other Item issue, one senior board member who has flown in from the US that same morning, asks the CEO, 'When is my taxi coming to pick me up for the airport?'

Finally, the last item on the agenda starts. The CEO presents his plans for engaging in a dialogue with a couple of private equity firms regarding the possible sale of one of the six remaining business areas, at least of one of the two separate units forming part of the business area. This is a plan that had come out of the strategy meeting that the group board had held during the meeting earlier in the spring. No decision has been made, however, the CEO has prepared a preliminary assessment of potential valuation of the business, and is asking the board to approve of the appointment of an investment bank to be in charge of the divestment process.

By the time the CEO finishes his presentation, the Chairman looks at his watch and has to finish the meeting. It is now 12:10 PM, and they are ten minutes late. One board member whose taxi had been ordered to pick him up at noon sharp, has already excused himself and left the meeting room.

The chairman announces the time and place of the next meeting, and the board meeting is concluded with his wishes for a great summer for everyone. Everybody leaves the head office of the company in a hurry.

Lessons to be learned

Reality case: 'A Morning in the Boardroom'

- Important and relevant material must be documented and distributed well in advance of the meeting.
- Only items pre-announced to the Chairman must be brought up during the board meeting session.
- Individual board members cannot be allowed to use the board for his/her agenda.
- Presentations by executive management must be focused and decision-oriented.
- Start the board meeting with 'Other Items' (at least to try it out).

CHAPTER 3
Enhancing the chairman's value

Although all corporations have a board, they can differ in structure and legal role according to their jurisdictions (two-tier structure, executives versus non-executives, union representation, and so on). All boards also have a chairman, but again with variations in role emphasis, which are regulated by differences in legislation, tradition, culture and other factors.

Oddly, relatively little academic research has been conducted around boards since Drucker in the 1950s emphasized their key roles in the book, *The Practice of Management*. Given the recent great turmoil and shakeout in the financial sector, this omission is surprising.

The research behind this book is based on conversations with forty-eight chairmen of large global corporations that have been conducted through in-depth interviews and long 'experience-sharing' discussions since early 2010. Topics discussed of relevance to all, both in and out of the boardroom, include the following:

- Should the chairman be given a more influential role in the overall governance and leadership of the corporation? If so, how should the appointment of the chairman be made so as to secure the right profile and skill base?
- What is the optimal profile and skill set for the chairman of a given corporation?
- Is the role of the chairman defined in an optimal way, if it is defined at all? If it is, does it allow the chairman to use their full potential?

- How can the chairman act so as to create strategic value for the corporation? What would be the best value levers for their active role?
- How should the chairman be compensated if they are being asked to take on a new and more active role that reflects their value contribution and acknowledges their exposure to liability should things go wrong?
- Is the chairman position emerging as a new and distinct profession?

There emerged a clear consensus amongst the chairmen, that they can add significantly more value to the companies they serve, but that this must be reflected in rethinking both how they are recruited and successfully retained, as well as how their roles and responsibilities should be defined.

There are arguments both for and against a reinforcement of the role of the chairman. The relationship with the CEO is a key issue in this respect. The research identified many examples where a well-functioning and complementary collaboration, which we call 'The Tandem' structure, have significantly enhanced the effectiveness of both strategic decision making and the execution of such decisions.

A five hour discussion with the chairman of one of the largest financial services groups in the world focused almost exclusively on the chairman role, 'This is the first time I have discussed these things with someone', he said. Then, he added, 'Who should I otherwise talk to? The CEO? No, he reports to me, and it does not feel right to ask him what I should or should not do'.

This research identifies the following key themes related to the role and challenges facing the chairman of the board:

1. **Top Leader:** The chairman is the 'Top Leader', the person put in charge to lead the work of the board and hence to be ultimately responsible for governance, the performance of the board, to be the face to the outside, and finally the person who has to make and execute the ultimate decision

to remove or replace the CEO. The latter being described by some as the key role of the chairman.

'The chairman only has one single important task to perform', said one chairman of a large financial conglomerate in Scandinavia, 'it is to fire the CEO'. Even if this certainly is a key task for the chairman, he/she should be given a more prominent leadership task in the corporation, and this leadership role should be defined and acknowledged throughout the organization. The leadership role goes beyond the pure role to chair board meetings and manage the Board of Directors; it implies strategic leadership for the entire corporation. The proposed leadership role leads to many issues, as is outlined in this section.

2. **Team Leader:** A second key role is described as being the 'Team Leader', or the coach and manager for the board team. The director responsible for seeing that the board works as a team and that the various skills and competencies of the individual board members are brought to bear on key tasks of the board. This role also leverages the potential that a diversity of background and skills of the board members could deliver.

3. **Governor Role:** A third and maybe a more traditional role, is the 'Governor Role', which is to be the company's spokesman to the world in matters of relationships, overall governance, and interaction with regulators/legislators. This is often the key role in large continental European corporations and is a legacy from past governance traditions.

   However, when used *in extremis*, such as for crisis management, it could have very negative effects unless coordinated and orchestrated by defined rules.

4. **Value Creator:** This is a key role where successful companies have found the right role for the chairman as a 'value creator', where they work with the rest of the board and the CEO and his team on key strategic issues to create value for the corporation. We see this in some cases where larger M&A deals were being pursued, in some major customer interactions (albeit this is an area where far too few chairmen or board members get involved), and, finally in cases

of an emerging crisis. To summarize, such actions tend to be too *ad hoc*, and both could and should be structured and planned in a much better way.

5. **'Tandem' Role:** This encompasses a successful dual approach to leadership, where the chairman and the CEO have defined and subsequently assigned key strategic roles to each other. The roles are explicit and by design, thereby playing on their relative strengths and core competencies. A combined chairman and CEO role is not generally acceptable or desirable, but remains a situation often found in U.S. corporations. At the same time a (too) strong chairman or CEO acting on their own is not desirable either. The ideal is a strong duo, a 'Tandem' at the top, where the chairman and the CEO work together in tandem to maximize synergies arising from complementary skills and competencies.

The chairman and the CEO in a large UK group had listed key tasks and decisions that required board approval, and then had divided up the responsibility for execution and follow-up between them. The assignment of roles was based on a profound discussion on relative skills and competencies. Acknowledging that he could not be the universal expert, the CEO had identified the strengths of his chairman that had been instrumental in establishing a new *modus operandi* between the two of them.

'We actually work as a great "Tandem", a team of two people who respect and trust each other, and we acknowledge both our strengths and weaknesses; it is a great partnership that I hope will last throughout my tenure at least', said the chairman of this UK corporation.

One key issue raised by many chairmen, as well as other board members, is the outdated nature of compensation for their services, dating back to when being appointed as chairman was a sign of honour and reward in itself, and the fundamental flaw arising from an asymmetric risk/reward structure in the compensation system. 'Why should I walk the extra mile for this company? There is really nothing in it for me, the more I get involved, the bigger the downside', as one chairman put it in a discussion.

The roles of the chairman: key challenges and opportunities

It is time to review and enhance the role of the chairman. We do not want to have a situation where an experienced and skilled executive with a vast personal network is assigned the role of chairing formal board meetings for two to four hours a handful of times per year, and signing protocols and reading from manuscripts produced by CFOs and Chief Legal Officers.

The following ideas and conclusions have been discussed with many of the chairmen interviewed for this book, and have thus been refined, made more realistic, and ready for implementation by corporations worldwide:

Define the key executive tasks for the chairman in a given corporation

Often such 'job/task descriptions' exist for the CEO, but write them down and agree on them also for the chairman. Clearly distinguish between what the tasks of the CEO are and those of the chairman respectively. Also, define what tasks belong to the entire board or its committees. Finally, align the CEO with the role descriptions for the chairman and communicate these explicitly for the top management team.

The chairman should be given the choice of accepting this active and executive-oriented role. This could require them to give up on an existing 'Old Boys Network' of members of the board.

Ask the chairman and the CEO to arrange specific tailor designed board strategy retreats

With both the C-level team involved, as well as with the board alone, define the core strategic tasks of the board. The purpose is twofold; to penetrate how to improve strategic performance and effectiveness of the board, as well as to create the kind of teamwork that so many chairmen requested during the research interviews. Such board retreats should be carefully prepared and focus on the key strategic issues where the board can get involved. This should not replace the strategic reviews that the board does where the CEO and the management team present the proposed strategy for the corporation; this is a key process that should be closely aligned with the board retreat itself. Then, make sure that future agendas for board meetings reflect these newly defined strategic roles and set a true strategic agenda for the board.

Define clearly the situations where the chairman can/shall act as a spokesman for the corporation

The general rule should be that the CEO is the company spokesman. However in some specific cases, where crisis management is required, the chairman can be assigned a role as part of the crisis management plan. But the task should be defined as to both scope and time. Only on very rare occasions should the chairman be called in to act as a 'crisis manager'.

Define the various strategic roles the board as well as the chairman should play in value creation for the corporation

There are examples where the chairman has been asked to share their network of contacts with the CEO and the management team, the excellent strategic initiatives this has resulted in, and where as a result real strategic value has been created for the corporation.

The role the chairman can play in supporting the CEO in creating commercial traction with new and existing key customers and strategic partners, as well as in major merger and acquisitions (M & A) situations must be noted. The new role associated in managing the emerging capital market players in the form of hedge funds and other activist investors cannot be underestimated. Here the chairman sometimes must embark on a learning process; these new phenomena in the capital markets have not always been fully digested and understood at the board level.

The Tandem concept is simple in theory; identify and define the core skills and potential contributions of the two leaders

The Tandem concept is easy in theory. But the trick is to define and assign them each the optimal set of such. This requires great leadership and personal skills to implement, from both the individuals involved. However, when being implemented in an optimal way, great examples of extraordinary results and success have been observed.

Both cultural and regulatory differences can make such a 'Tandem' structure almost impossible to implement successfully. But when possible and whenever the two leaders at the top jointly agree to form such a duo, it should be carefully considered. It must be a joint initiative with a full consensus on division of tasks and roles.

The emerging new chairman profession

Without exception, all chairmen agreed that the role of the chairman should be enhanced and defined as a key resource for the corporation as a whole. They also agreed that it should be recognized and defined as a new profession with all the requirements for qualifications that go with a leadership role.

This implies a new definition of the chairman as a distinct and recognized profession. The requirements of the fast-moving globalized world need a new generation of chairmen who take this as an inspiring profession from the age of 50 plus and who want to write a new chapter in sustainable, value-creating, corporate governance.

In many countries, enough rules and regulations have been established in order to generate prosperity through corporations. The discipline is established, now we need a highly professional, energizing, and value-creating part of excellent corporate governance.

In summary, this leads to:

- A new recruiting policy and strategy for the chairman's position.
- Adequate training and development for taking on the job of the Top Leader.
- A compensation system which is 'symmetric', that is, aligns rewards for performance and balances the system between risk and return.
- A clearly defined 'job description' for the chairman of what his/her tasks are and what lies outside the scope of this work.
- A mutual understanding and 'bond' between the chairman and the CEO.
- Assign key roles between the CEO and chairman.
- A firm commitment from the chairmen themselves; no individual could carry out more than a limited number of these tasks.

These recommendations and concepts cannot be implemented everywhere. Old traditions and many regulatory constraints still exist in some markets and regions. However, it is always the case that 'Good Can Be Done Better'.

Reality case

The new chairman takes charge

'The First Year on the Job' Plan

An executive has just been appointed as the new chairman of a food production group. It is one of the country's largest corporations, so she is very excited over the new engagement and her tasks to oversee a major strategic transformation of the group. She had been carefully selected by the largest owner, who also has a separate interest in the food sector in addition to ownership of a large portfolio of holdings in many sectors both at home and abroad.

The largest owner had insisted on a major strategic overhaul of the group and had a clear view on what the goals for the long-term future should be. The new chairman had been told that her main task would be to lead the forthcoming strategic change program. But, first, she and the owner had worked together to find a new CEO for the group. Once the CEO had been hired, in a jointly conducted recruiting process, the new chairman had come onboard. She had committed to spend up to half of her time on the new position for one year, working very closely with the CEO in the transformation process.

The rest of the board remained partly intact, but the owner made no secret of the fact that they were looking at a major reorganization of the board as well. First things first, they had told him. The incoming chairman had been spending quite a lot of time preparing for the new job. It reminded her of the first time she had been appointed CEO for an IT company. She had been asked by the owner to consider her engagement as the new chairman in the same way that she had been briefed before coming on as the CEO in the past.

Therefore, she had written down the first set of action priorities in a form of manifest that she had presented to the owner and subsequently, at least in parts, to the board at the first board meeting and then to each of the board members one by one.

It started with the imperative to establish a well-defined working relationship with the new CEO. She believed this should be a good time to establish such rules of engagement as they were both new on their respective positions.

The two of them spent a weekend together, testing out different definitions of their roles and tasks. At the end of the long meeting, they both felt comfortable that the way they had divided key tasks and responsibilities would work well.

Enhancing the chairman's value

The chairman went on to define the other key elements of her first year on the job. She called it 'The First Year Plan', and spent significant time in preparing and then presenting the plan to the owner and the board. The first joint initiative with the CEO and the board was to initiate a strategy review with an international consulting firm. The chairman called the project a 'Strategic Appraisal'.

It involved a close collaboration with the management team, something the chairman saw as almost as important as the analytical work. It gave her a good opportunity to interact with the management team on the job. The result of the appraisal was a revised new strategic plan for the group.

Based on the consultants' recommendations, the chairman set up a plan for implementation and the overall responsibility for implementing this plan was assigned to the CEO and his team. The chairman was asked to support the team in certain key partnership discussions as well as in preparing for a set of proposed acquisitions of local competitors in Europe as well as the implementation of a new distribution structure in the US market.

But the major part of her time as the new chairman was spent on communicating with the rest of the board and with the outside world. She and the CEO had divided responsibility for communication between themselves. The chairman was overall responsible for communicating what they together had defined as extraordinary events and issues, whereas the CEO was in charge for presenting and commenting on of major new strategic initiatives. The focus was on establishing credibility for the new top structure.

Lessons to be learned

Reality case: 'The New Chairman takes Charge'

- The process of finding and attracting the new Chairman should be as robust and structured as for hiring key executives.

- The role of the Chairman required a very significant commitment of time and effort to the task assigned.
- The Chairman must establish a good and effective 'Modus Vivendi' both with the owner, the rest of the board, as well as with the CEO and his/her top team.
- The Chairman should set clearly defined goals and define 'Deliverables' for his/her work (and align these with owner and board expectations).

CHAPTER 4

Chairman and CEO: tandem at the top

> I had the best possible board and my CEO had a wonderful team around him; but we could not work in harmony together. One of us had to leave. I stayed, he left, and now the board and the entire top organization is working extremely well as one team. It was sad but necessary to part ways.

This quote, from one of the chairmen interviewed for this research, shows in essence what almost all of them expressed as the key issue for effectiveness of the board and for top-level value creation in their organizations. The research indicates in favour of having a pair of leaders at the top working together – where both leaders are leveraging from each other's core skills and competencies. This is the 'Tandem' at the top. This implies that they work together but have chosen different roles and have agreed on a division of key tasks between them.

Peter Drucker wrote, 'Every case of business growth is the achievement of at least two men working together' (Drucker, 1969). He added, 'The concept of the one-man CEO is contrary to all experience and to the demands of the job. If applied, it leads to trouble.'

As mentioned, few academics have spent significant time and effort researching this key relationship, albeit it exists in almost all corporations worldwide. In most countries today, we find a split of the chairman and CEO role into two distinct positions. Thus, the issue of defining a well-functioning relationship between the two has become highly relevant for almost all companies.

A recent study by Kakabadse and Kakabadse (2006) supports the view that the chairman and CEO relationship is a key element of any successful organizational and managerial structure. As a chairman of a large Indian conglomerate explained to me, 'The relationship between the two of us at the top, is the most important of all; when it works well, you have a self-playing piano. And this piano is playing music that is creating huge value for the shareholders.'

'Tandem' leadership

Tandem Leadership implies that the two leaders work together as a pair, where each one is assigned roles and responsibilities that best fit with his/her core skills and competencies. Drucker (1955) makes the comparison with a tennis doubles team. He writes, 'In playing doubles tennis each player has an area of responsibility; but he is also expected to cover his partner... the partners in collaboration work out the lines of demarcation themselves. To play a winning doubles game a team must have played together quite a bit; but once the partners have come to know and to trust each other there will be no gaps on their side of the net.'

Here we list them as they have been expressed during the discussions with chairmen and CEOs respectively:

- To create a winning 'doubles team' or the 'Tandem', the two top leaders must complement each other, both as to skills but also as to personality.
- A good personal chemistry is imperative, but the relationship must not become too personal. At all times, professional standards must apply. The 'Old Boys Network' must not reappear in a disguised Tandem version.
- The key tasks and responsibilities must be carefully defined and assigned to each of the leaders so as best to fit his/

her profile of skills and competencies. It should be documented and accepted by both and get a final approval from the board. The CEO should inform his management team about the agreement and be prepared to discuss the implications of the dual leadership with them.
- The tandem structure must not interfere with the CEO's reporting structure and 'chain of command' versus his/her top level managers. The chairman must never bypass the CEO and start managing the line of executives.
- Equally important, the CEO must not aim at imposing him/herself on the board, but leave the chair of the board meetings to the chairman.
- The key success factor for a Tandem to be effective is that both leaders show each other mutual respect, and that there is a strong bond between them based on mutual trust.
- Both chairman and CEO must have access to accurate and relevant information to support their jobs. The chairman must have full access to such information through a well defined and structured process.

As one of the chairmen said, 'We are good friends, of course, but we had to draw a line in the sand; where friendship stops and business takes over. We have sworn to each other never to mix the two. It is hard sometimes, but it works if professionalism prevails between equals. And in our case, it does. After work, we can go skiing together, or just go out for a beer.'

Key issues for a successful 'tandem'

The key aspect of the Tandem has been previously listed, *mutual trust and respect*. But successful teams are not created by themselves, at least not in large corporations. There are several factors that tend to come up during the duration of the Tandem relationship. Here are some of the more important:

1. Forming the Tandem
    - When searching for the two leaders to be selected for the top positions, the board must start with these

questions: What kind of leaders does this corporation need? What are the key strategic challenges facing the business going forward? What leadership skills are required to create the value inherent in the business? Are we in for growth/restructuring?
- Most of the time, the board starts with at least one of the positions already filled by a competent executive. Assuming the skill set and profile of this leader is adequate, the search must be initiated to find his/her partner.
- Political and other sub-optimal considerations must be set aside; only competence should count in the selection of the Tandem partner. And no 'Old Boys Network' thinking must be allowed to influence any such decision.
- The two potential partners must be asked to meet and be informed about the dual leadership role. Then, they should discuss whether the proposed Tandem could be an attractive proposition for them. If one of them is not onboard for such a solution, the process must be rethought and another partner candidate found; one who accepts the Tandem role.

2. Assigning the tasks and responsibilities
- Most experienced leaders know what is required from them in a certain executive position. The two partners should thus be able to define the shared tasks and responsibilities themselves.
- A key imperative is that both leaders must accept, and understand the rationale not to interfere in one another's defined responsibilities and roles.
- The chairman is the CEO's boss; this must be made clear at all times. But the 'rules of engagement' must be well defined. What precisely does this command structure imply? And what should be left to the board and/or the board's dedicated committees, such as the Compensation Committee, Nomination Committee and so on?
- Some of the areas where the Tandem should work as a team are:
  - Larger M&A transactions: Here a two-man negotiating team is always a major advantage; all executives that

have been involved in top level negotiations embrace the two people team structure to help achieve extraordinary outcomes.
- Crisis management: Experience shows the imperative imbedded in the choice of one spokesman to external parties.
- Capital market interaction: This is another area where the Tandem partners should define exactly who is doing what. New phenomena such as activist and hedge funds put an extra pressure on the top team to adapt a clearly defined channel for such communication; do nothing is not a viable alternative.
- Strategic customer and partner acquisition and management: As for M&A deals, the approach to successful closing of major strategic opportunities should also be subject to a sharing between the two leaders at the top.

'I always ask my chairman to come with me to major customer meetings; he knows the market space and is a respected captain of industry. With him and me together, we dramatically enhance our chances of achieving successful outcomes from such customer discussions and negotiations. I can count numerous such commercial successes that we could attribute to our teamwork,' said one of the CEOs interviewed for this book.

3. Information sharing
   - The chairman and the CEO must have access to all relevant information. A specifically defined set of data should be provided to the chairman on a timely basis. He/she does not need and should not have access to all management information reported to the CEO and the management team.
   - A specifically defined reporting system should be set up to provide the chairman with such data.
   - In addition, the chairman should have the right to request additional information on a 'by need' basis. However, based on the experience shared with the chairmen and

CEOs in this research study, specific routines must be established for this incremental reporting process.
4. Termination and succession procedures when parting ways
   - As for all key positions in a corporation, there must be a plan for the chairman's succession.
   - The stronger the Tandem has been working together, the more delicate the succession becomes, thus requiring a defined plan for this event.
   - It should be noted, that in some countries, the chairman's tenure is defined by law and sometimes limited in time.
   - Also, a chairman, as a board member, could always be replaced by the shareholders at a general meeting under most versions of modern corporate law.
   - Finally, it is the ultimate task and duty of the chairman to terminate the contract for the CEO, should the circumstances require such a decision. As for any boss, it is then the chairman's duty to execute this decision and terminate the CEO contract.
   - This is one of the key reasons for why the Tandem partners must be able to separate their professional relation from any personal bond of friendship that may arise between them.
5. Interacting with the board
   - Both the CEO and the chairman would have different roles *vis-à-vis* the board and should be assigned different reporting requirements for board meetings.
   - It was strongly recommended by almost all the chairmen and the CEOs interviewed for this book, that the agenda is put together by both leaders; bearing in mind that the agenda *de facto* defines the role of the board and its role in strategic decision making and so on.
   - But proposals to the board must be made by the CEO, even if he/she and the chairman already have agreed on the proposal.
   - And all relevant information for such decision making must be made available to the board members. To keep privileged information between the two Tandem partners is 'against the rules of the game' and is a strong recipe for disaster.

Major benefits of the tandem

When a well-functioning Tandem relationship is in place, it typically leads to a number of positive effects for the organization and the underlying business success, primarily from the following:

- An effective and value creating board.
- Regardless of the qualities of the other board members, without the duo at the top working together, it will have negative impact on the board as a whole.
- The Tandem creates lots of incremental value in matters as previously outlined.
- Managerial synergies at the top where the best qualities of the two top leaders can be leveraged for value creation for the company.
- Good balance between executive management and board.

But these positive effects do not come by themselves. They require a careful and systematic approach to finding and attracting the right candidate for both the chairman as well as the CEO position. Of great priority is to establish the 'rules of engagement' for the Tandem as well as the 'lines of demarcation' that Drucker referred to.

Again, the differences in the legal structure between different jurisdictions make a Tandem solution more or less viable. It is particularly attractive in the Scandinavian/Swiss system with a one-tier board and where typically the chairman and the CEO are two different positions upheld by two different individuals. But it could work also in the Anglo-Saxon system with executives and non-executives as board directors. Finally, also under a two-tier structure, we have seen examples of working Tandem pair solutions.

But even the best of Tandem solutions can be damaged by too much shareholder politics and in-fighting. The research highlighted several very happy Tandem partners who expressed their comfort with the well-functioning and balanced relationship.

But as in any marriage, it takes an effort by both parties to work to maintain an amicable and at the same time professional modus operandi between the two individuals involved.

Why a combined chairman and CEO role is *not* a viable solution

Turning to the notion of blending the two roles into one; this is still common practice in some countries, predominantly in the United States and in France, where 80 per cent of chairmen also serve as the CEO (in France, the combined role is that of the President Directeur Générale, PDG). In most other countries, the role is split, such as in the United Kingdom in over 90 per cent of the companies reported (Coombes & Wong, 2004), and in some countries, such as Russia and Japan, in 100 per cent of corporations.

If, in addition, the remaining directors are non-executive or independent, the combined chairman and CEO has a huge information advantage, and the board meetings sometimes become a pure information gathering session, where the chairman/CEO communicates already decided upon (and, in some cases, even already implemented) issues. This has led to some major corporate failures in the recent past. We recommend shareholders, who ultimately decide on the issue, to avoid this mixing of roles and positions going forward.

Reality case

The chairman and CEO Tandem

They were very good friends; in fact they had just returned from a weekend of skiing together. Now they agreed to meet for breakfast at a hotel restaurant near the head office building of the bank where they both worked. It is early in the morning, and the two are almost alone in the otherwise crowded restaurant, seated in the far corner of the room.

Chairman and CEO: tandem at the top

The two meet regularly for discussion of progress and specific issues that both sent to the other by e-mail the evening before their reunions. They grouped the issues into five categories: 'Strategic', 'Operations', 'People', 'Key Business Issues', and 'Personal Issues'. Typically, they tried to meet twice per month, often in a private setting but always well prepared along the previous lines.

They both felt that they complemented each other very well. The chairman had a long career in industry himself. He had been a member of the board of another bank in the past, but this specific engagement was his only board directorship at the moment. The CEO had spent most of his professional career in banking, so he had the deep industry knowledge.

The chairman often joked that his lack of in-depth knowledge of banking made him a better leader for the board. 'I can ask the simple and seemingly stupid questions that nobody dare to ask' he used to say to the CEO. 'But only because you know me; most other CEO's would have gone through the roof if they heard somebody displaying such obvious lack of insight in my position!'

This morning they had a delicate issue to discuss; the previous day, one major daily paper had published an article that claimed that the bonus for the CEO for last year was going to be raised by almost 50 per cent. This kind of 'scoop' was not uncommon at all, particularly not after the results of the financial crisis. Their particular bank had not been hurt as severely as some of the others, but badly enough for the public opinion to cry out for 'blood money' and similar popular demands.

The truth was that the issue of the bonus had not yet been decided upon and any plans to award a bonus or variable performance-based compensation was supposed to be limited to the chairman and the selected members of the bank's Compensation Committee. Some other board members had given their opinion on the issue to the chairman but he had as of yet not taken any action and no decision had been made.

In fact, the two had already begun the discussion of the yearly compensation last year. The Compensation Committee, of which the chairman was a member but not its chair person, had raised the issue of whether the existing bonus system based on the bank's performance should be kept. It was argued that so many external factors had come into play, affecting the results and performance of the bank. For example, the new Basel III rules, the consequences of which were still to be seen and defined.

In addition, the increasing pressure on banks to hold back on extraordinary compensation was clearly affecting the thinking amongst many members of the board. In fact, some members of the Compensation Committee wanted to abandon performance-based variable compensation altogether. The chairman had so far resisted this plan.

The chairman had asked the CEO to present his view of the situation and a proposal for how, in principle, the compensation structure should be designed going forward. They began the morning meeting by agreeing that the situation was of extraordinary nature due to the obvious leak of information from the boardroom or its surroundings. But that nevertheless, any solution they agreed upon must be sustainable and be fair and in line with the bank's values and rules.

The CEO suggested that they would increase the fixed portion of the salary by 15 per cent and then base a small variable compensation part on the part of the bank's profits that resulted from the bank's own core operations. They also agreed that this latter element must be transparent and communicated to all relevant stakeholders, including the media.

'This is the way we would do it in the retail industry,' the chairman stated. 'It must work in banking also,' the CEO declared.

They finished their breakfast and agreed to meet again in two weeks' time.

Lessons to be learned

Reality case: 'The Chairman & CEO Tandem'

- The skills and competence of the two top leaders should complement each other.
- The relationship between Chairman and CEO is key for a functioning corporate governance.
- If the relationship does not work, one of the two must leave.

CHAPTER 5

The owner and the board

'I am here to execute the intent and directions set by the Owner,' one Chairman said during the interview. 'But I do not know who the owner is; he has no face and hardly any voice. Rather the Owner is a group of institutional investors and they are represented by their appointed investment managers. They never tell me where they want to take the company; in fact they are just concerned about our returns and risk levels.'

This is an extraordinary remark, because the board is defined as being the mandated representative for the owner, the shareholder (-s). Therefore, the Chairman, being the leader of the board, should be the key counterpart for any key discussions with the owner he/she represents, on strategy and direction for the corporation. But this Chairman, who is chairing the board of a large European industrial group, is not alone in his search for a face and a voice with whom to discuss. This phenomenon, where there is a lack of a clearly identified owner who is tangible and present, is indeed one of the issues most chairmen and senior board members raised with me during the long discussions we have had during my work.

Obviously, this is a situation that is related to the publicly listed companies whose stock is trading on the stock exchange, and where institutional ownership has become a standard rather than an exception. However, the relationship between the board and the owner is an often overlooked issue in the management literature.

Corporate law in most countries defines the general rules for corporate governance. But the fact that the board is elected by the shareholders at the general meeting and thus is given a mandate to represent them and act in their best interest is the general rule. Thus, the law leaves the board very much in a position to define how specifically this representation and mandate should be executed. As a result, we find that attempts have been made to define such 'codes of conduct' and 'Board Instructions'.

The reality is that the only interaction between the owner/shareholder and the board as defined by the law is to be carried out at the Shareholders Meeting, whether general or extraordinary. Therefore, the trust in corporate governance is profound. This is the general philosophy behind the corporate law and this definition of governance; the owner/shareholder appoints the board and the board appoints the chairman. But, typically, the latter decision is returned to shareholders for final approval.

The legal means left to the shareholders to impose their will on the board, and thus implicitly on the management of the corporation, is the ability to call a shareholder meeting and replace the board. In reality today, many directors are voted in for a specific period of time, terms typically ranging from one to several years. Thus, the owner must have a very serious and well-founded reason to revoke the mandate of a board member. In addition, s/he must also have power to control the necessary majority required by the local corporate law or company charters in question.

There is a difference in a family-owned enterprise, where a family or a foundation fully controls the corporation. Even so, we all have seen examples where family-owned companies become a battleground for infighting fractions of various parts of the owner family. Thus, the board has been the frontline for such internal family 'wars'.

During my time as Director of Bain & Company, I sometimes found myself working for and reporting to the CEO and board of large state-owned enterprises. During my research, I also interviewed the chairmen of a few of those.

The general notion and sentiment of the chairmen of such national assets seem to be that there should be no difference between leading state-owned corporations and privately held dittos. This is probably correct when it comes to the conduct of the core business processes with some notable exceptions. But the chairmen pointed at the closer interaction with the state owner, represented through the Government. Therefore, despite the criticism and questioning of state ownership we find many times in media and politics, the reality seems to indicate that the state as an owner de facto does take on an active role and interacts with the board. This has an impact on the strategy and direction of the corporation. The critic would argue that this is all fine, but the real issue is whether the quality and relevance of such interactions and briefings is adequate and good enough. This is not the forum for such a more philosophical debate, although I believe most regard the issue as being highly relevant.

To conclude, the nature and execution of ownership does have an impact on the relationship between the owner and the board. Therefore, relationship could be argued on the long-term strategy of the corporation and its impact also on the strategic mandate of the board. I return to this in the following paragraphs.

Let us turn to a set of key issues related to the owner and the relation with the board.

The lack of direct ownership

As the chairman previously notes, one of the key issues is the lack of a 'real' owner, with his/her own 'flesh and blood (and brain)'. This is a phenomenon that has increased in magnitude during the second half of the last century and the beginning of the twenty-first century. Private owners, whether large or

The owner and the board

small, have to a large extent been replaced by a set of anonymous owners; the institutional investors such as pension funds, asset and wealth managers, and more recent phenomena such as hedge funds and even private equity ownership. In addition, small shareholders are now partly acting as 'day traders' and 'stock pickers' who fundamentally have no or little interest in the long-term sustainability of corporate strategy or goals.

How has the board, the owner's mandated representative, chosen to deal with this situation? One Chairman told this interesting and insightful story:

> I am chairing two companies; one is partly controlled by a family foundation, so I am used to having regular and very interactive meetings with the representative of the foundation. We would discuss most matters of strategy and in our case ethics and sustainability of our business and mission. I spend many hours preparing and analysing these meetings.

The Chairman went on to say:

> The other company has no large private owner. There are seven different institutions that together control a little over 50% of the capital and thus the votes; no one of them holds over 10%. They have chosen one of their investment managers to represent them all in the communication with me and the board. We meet ahead of the annual shareholder meeting to discuss possible new board members, etc. This person would also call me after we publish our results if he has any additional information requests or wants clarification.

He added:

> We also discuss the staffing and duties of the committees, particularly the compensation and audit committees. I understand that this is the way the institutions must

> operate, and it is OK with me. But we never discuss strategy. Not to mention operations. Honestly, sometimes I wonder if the board members representing the institutions even know anything substantial about the specific industry we are operating in. Or if they even care! But if we have missed the profit target by a few percentage points, then he is very active and sometimes tough to handle. The institutions alter the role between them, but the representative is always a member of the present board. To chair these two boards is living on different planets; but actually both work, even if I prefer the face to face meetings with a 'real owner'.

This latter situation is a reality for many boards today. Often, the interaction with the institutional owners is limited to formal reporting and interaction through committee work. Even if the same institutions play a part in nominating and appointing new board members, these board members do not carry with them a clear and explicit mandate for strategic direction and long-term goals for the company.

The second comment by the Chairman referred to previously is even more worrying. Is the owner's representative lacking relevant knowledge and understanding of the underlying business the company is engaged in? If so, is there enough motivation on behalf of the owner representative, typically an investment manager employed by the fund, to truly engage in the ongoing concern he/she is mandated to govern? Is this perhaps one of the key reasons why we have seen the serious mismanagement of many boards in the recent crisis? Not at least looking at what was emerging from the collapse of the financial services sector. Since the connection between an owner's lack of understanding with potential mismanagement of the board is such an important topic on its own, I will further elaborate on it later in this chapter.

The chairman's description of the absent owner is thus something we must bear in mind when discussing the role of the board in strategic value creation and leadership. It has implications for what and how we should expect board members to act and behave.

The virtues of the active owner

As is the case with the nature of ownership, direct versus indirect, private versus publicly listed, state versus privately owned, family and foundation owned, and so on, the degree of active ownership varies widely between corporations.

Based on the findings from my research, and also from my own experience, it can be argued that the role of the board varies with the degree of active involvement from the owner.

In listed companies where there is at least one strong private shareholder, many times this owner takes on a more active role in the governance of the corporation. For example, in private equity, the board of a portfolio company is the key element for strategic coordination and control of the business. The role of the board in a family-owned company also becomes different and the research shows that many times the board has been given a very active role in strategy implementation.

A clear role of very active ownership is the role of the Founder in the early stage ventures. The Founder and owner controls the company by the virtue of both his/her know-how of the business, but also through a controlling ownership stake. Over time, however, we typically see how the founder's role changes, mostly because of the gradual dilution of his/her ownership through new capital injections into the business by external investors.

Active ownership tends to focus on long-term strategy and drivers of value creation. This leads to a more prominent role of the board in such strategic value creation processes. I have worked extensively with private equity firms, both as advisor and board member in portfolio companies. As we have seen not least in recent public debates, the private equity industry has been accused of a short-term focus and lack of sustainability in their choice of business models and asset allocation decisions. However, I still argue that most corporations have much to learn by studying the core elements of the active ownership often performed by private equity firms. Yes, there is a difference in the time scale used, with the fund structure and rules calling for an exit from the investment within a certain period of time, typically between three to five years.

Nevertheless, the way private equity firms approach value creation is many times 'best practice' that could be adapted by corporations acting under a different ownership paradigm. This active owner approach also affects the design of corporate governance and hence the role of the board.

The board in many private equity-owned companies is a key tool for execution of active ownership and strategy. The Modus Operandi of these boards, could, at least in relevant parts, be adapted by boards in other corporations. This could be a leveraged topic for new and subsequent research on the role of the board.

One could argue that a similar situation can be found in the subsidiaries of large corporations, especially in the board of group subsidiaries, both in domestic and foreign dittos. This was one of the main focus areas, when I studied the boards in foreign subsidiaries of large multinational companies together with Dr. Laurent Leksell in 1982. Results of the research were published in *Journal of International Business Studies*, 1982.

Our findings showed that successful groups defined clear roles for their foreign subsidiary boards. Subsequently, they composed them to reflect these same roles and responsibilities. The best practice was characterized by assigning clearly defined roles to the external board members, many times being prominent members of the local business communities and as such with access to valuable close networks.

Translation of owner's vision and goals into corporate strategy

Years ago, when I was one of the senior partners of the firm I had co-founded with two of my friends and fellow Ph.D. colleagues, one of the first assignments we had was a strategy consultant for a family-owned group that had grown into a highly diversified conglomerate during the 1970s and early 1980s. Our small firm had been engaged by the management team to conduct a review of long-term corporate strategy of the group. We were both proud and happy for this highly prestigious assignment and conducted a review of the portfolio of businesses of the client. We came to the conclusion and recommendation that the family-owned group should concentrate on its core business, and, as a result, divest of its non-media assets. The partners were asked to present the results to the Chairman of the group with only a few selected members of management present.

After our presentation (this was before the era of PowerPoint and computer graphics), and having given our recommendations to the Chairman and management, the Chairman rose from the table and told us the following:

> You have got this all wrong! I really should not pay your bill (the payment of which was of critical importance to our young and growing firm; my comment). Because you have not understood the virtue of the strategy we have pursued.

He went on and added:

> However, as your results and recommendations have some merit in a ore generic sense, I will pay your bill. But not implement your recommendations. You see, my responsibility as the chairman of this family business, is to manage the future wealth and legacy of this family. The fundamental reason for our strategy and structure, is a result of

> diversification of risk and thus to accept a slightly lower return. ... Next time, my Boys [he always referred to us as 'Boys'; he was almost eighty years old at the time but full of life and energy and extremely strong as leader], you should spend ample time to get the correct brief of the owner of the business you are to analyze and recommend strategy for. But remember to do so before you set out to use your analytical skills and expertise as advisors. Never forget that!

We never forgot that. In fact, it could have meant the final day of our aspiring and young enterprise. There are significant lessons to be learned from this episode, not only for professional advisors such as consulting firms, investment banks, lawyers and others, but most certainly for board members.

Another interesting example is based on the experiences of senior board member of a large family-controlled publicly listed group in Asia.

> We have made the board the key instrument in communicating the values and strategic goals of our group. This is the most important strategic goal we define; that every business in our group should be embraced by our core values and virtues. In fact, we systematically review the portfolio of the group (the company is highly diversified; my comment). Businesses found not to meet our core value criteria will be divested.

The senior board member added:

> It is the primary task of the boards in the various businesses to communicate and translate these values and virtues, that are many times of ethical nature, and therefore sometimes a bit complex to define and understand for management. But it works and we spend a lot of time carefully selecting and educating our board members to fully understand these values and rules.

These are two examples where the owner was playing an active role in formulation and communication of vision and overall strategic direction for the company. Another interesting example of such direct involvement of the owner is the way a large Asian industrial group is pursuing its global operations. As one board member in the group described it:

> Every employee in our group has got to sign up for the code of conduct that we apply to everything we do. This is particularly true for our corporate social responsibility. I dare to say that in our case this is not just putting nice words on our website, but the values illustrated in the code is a fact of everyday life at work for the entire organization. Today over two hundred thousand employees have signed the code and promised to adapt its principles in his/her work processes, regardless of level and reporting structure. The role of the parent company is to communicate and explain the meaning of the values so expressed. This is where the boards in the group play a vital role. It has to come from the top; we have to live as we teach as they say.

But how does this play out in the world of the 'Zombie Owners'?

Modus vivendi: interaction between owner and board

As can be seen from the preceding, there are some very good examples of how the owner can interact with the representatives who have been given a mandate to safeguard and develop the interests of the shareholder/owner. But we have also seen the overwhelming number of situations where the board has no owner to interact with, or rather where the owner is an unknown or anonymous institution represented by an investment manager or a 'Board Pro'.

This situation of the 'ownerless' corporation is a real problem in today's corporate world. Many of the world's largest corporations could be classified as being 'ownerless', that is, without a strong and recognized owner who could take an active role in determining the long-term direction and goals for the company.

There were also a few examples of what one chairman called the 'Board Bypass'. It is worth mentioning as it is not a unique case of 'cheating' with corporate governance procedures. He explained the situation as follows:

> I have noticed that our CEO has a very active dialogue with the representatives for a few of our major institutional owners. They are discussing various strategic initiatives, and I assume the CEO gets good advice from this New York based investment fund. The access to wall Street and an active deal flow is of course always positive. But I am not so fond of the fact that the CEO spends more and more time with some of the owners than with me and the rest of the board. In fact, a few weeks ago he told me that the owner representative, a senior investment manager, had asked him if we were prepared to engage in a merger discussion with one of our strategic partners. The idea is probably very good for development of our business, but I find it less appropriate that this discussion is held outside of the board as a whole. This particular investment manager has been the fund's board representative for quite a long time, but nonetheless, this time I believe our CEO has gone too far. I told him so but he did not seem to agree. I think we have a problem here.

The situation described reinforces the importance of establishing a defined structure and process for the interaction between the board and the owner as well as how this relationship impacts the entire governance structure and procedures. Let us turn to this subject now.

First, it is through my own experience and was also confirmed during the research that the most common form for interaction between owner and board is to assign a liaison task to the

Chairman. With the exception for the rules associated with the shareholder meetings, there are no regulatory rules for how the Chairman should manage this interaction nor how and when it should take place.

One Chairman had this view:

> About a month in advance to the annual shareholder meeting, I write a brief note to the major owners. I give them a personal summary of the state of the corporation and point out if there are any key issues that I intend to bring up at the forthcoming general meeting. I then have a time set up for a ten to fifteen minutes conference call with the owner or his representative. In my letter I have asked them to prepare issues and questions that they want to raise with me at the call. Unless they bring up some extraordinary or totally unexpected question, we normally have time to sort them out during the call. But it could happen that they ask for a special meeting with me if the issue at hand is of major importance to the corporation. Then I would also inform the other board members about the fact of course. This works very well.

In many companies, the traditional solution to let the Chairman act as the 'liaison' between owner and board has been complemented by a more comprehensive structure involving others in addition to the Chairman.

Through my interviews and discussions with board members and CEOs, some interesting patterns emerged of how such an active dialogue and interaction between the owner and the board could be designed and managed. This also showed how the owner and the board could be aligned with the overall governance principles and procedures.

We turn now to some of these examples as they may give some ideas for thought and clarify how a fruitful relationship could work.

The 'Presidium'

The first example comes from a large European group with a diversified portfolio of large holdings that also pursues a very active ownership involving direct involvement at board level in the various group companies. Typically, the group appoints a couple of the board members, including one director who is being given a more specific mandate to follow the strategy and operations of the company on behalf of the owner. This designated director then forms the third member of what within the group is being referred to as the 'Presidium'.

In addition to the owner's designated director, the Presidium also consists of the chairman and the CEO. Typically, the Presidium meets regularly in advance of the board meetings. They have been given the same notice and information as the rest of the board, but at the meeting of the Presidium that precedes the actual board meeting, most or all of the key decision-making items are discussed. No formal decisions are made, of course, but the issues are discussed and the suggested options 'vetted' ahead of the actual meeting. The board meets shortly thereafter, typically on the same or the following day.

> 'I am happy with the Presidium solution,' a CEO in one of the companies said during an interview. 'It gives me a good platform to present my plans in advance to the board meetings, and I get instant feedback on how the Board would probably look at the proposals. We are very careful so as not to isolate the erst of the Board from the process. I take a special task on myself to keep them informed about the same issues we are discussing during the Presidium meetings. It works and I am sure it is a very effective way of enhancing the quality of decision-making.'

The 'TROIKA'

Another example is similar to the 'Presidium' solution. It is used by EQT, a Swedish-based private equity group, for the governance of its portfolio companies and is called the 'TROIKA'. It also consists of the CEO, the Chairman and one partner from the private equity firm management company.

The role of the TROIKA is to prepare the board meetings but also to act as a forum for the CEO to bring up and discuss ideas not yet ready for presentation to the board as a whole. The existence of the TROIKA is well known throughout the group and works very well. The members of the TROIKA work closely together and meet frequently as a group in between board meetings.

EQT points out that the TROIKA is not a substitute for the board meetings. It should only act as a forum for interaction between the owners and the company. The TROIKA concept and Modus Operandi is outlined in the following Reality Case EQT.

TROIKA has been designed for a private equity structure, but my own experience is that many of the solutions we find in private equity could be transferred to a corporate situation after some adjustments. In fact, the TROIKA solution is very similar to some of the other designs of board and owner interaction that was found in other corporations as well. This is shown in the following section.

The chairman committee

The chairman of a large Central European bank shared the following about his chosen model for owner interaction:

> I have organized a small group consisting of myself, the CEO, our CFO and one board member whom I have asked to represent the largest owners of the bank. This is what we call the Chairman Committee. We met for to hours in advance to all board meetings and ahead of the shareholder meeting. It is a recognized committee that shows the same kind of transparency as the other committees. In reality, most strategic and other key issues are being

discussed in the committee before being brought up at the main board meetings. We found this to be a very good way to ee to that all major strategic decisions have been vetted and accepted by the largest owners and that there is an acceptance for them at the executive management level as well. Everybody is happy with this structure and we have seen great improvements in the effectiveness and accuracy of decision-making at the board level as a result.

He went on to add:

However, there is one very important aspect of this committee structure and I am spending much time in explaining this to the rest of the board; the Chairman Committee must never become a substitute for the real board. And it must not create an 'elite clique' of board members. Because it is obviously so that the members of this committee will have access to more information and earlier information than the rest of the board members. However, this is always the case for all committee members. Just look at the discussions and information flow going to the Risk and Compensation Committees! So we have agreed that the discussions and outcomes of Chairman Committee meetings are just part of the normal governance procedures and processes in our bank. All shareholders are aware of the fact that we have this committee and no one has ever objected to it. I have also made it clear that the two board members representing the owners must take care of all owners' interest, not just the largest with whom they have a direct and active dialogue in between the board meetings. And that no proprietary and classified information is provided to just a few of the shareholders. This process has been carefully vetted and approved of our auditors and the general meeting as well.

The Chairman Committee structure was observed in several of the corporations that took part in the research. They sometimes adapt quite 'bold' names, such as in the case of an Italian media group, 'The Central Council', and in one large Brazilian group, 'The Corporate Strategy Centre'. In a Swedish industrial group, the equivalent name was simply 'The Strategy Committee'.

The owner liaison director

A variation of the previous themes with committee or group structures is what I experienced in one French industrial group. It should be noted that in France, the traditional solution to the governance structure found in most other European countries is similar to what we see in many US corporations. In both cases, the chairman and the CEO is one and the same position, or what in French is referred to as the 'President Directeur Général' or 'PDG' in short.

In the case of this publicly listed multi-billion euro group, the PDG had selected one of the board directors to represent the largest owner of the company; this shareholder controlled over 30 per cent of the capital that was the remainder of the founder family holdings. The family office had kept a close control of the group during the three generations that had superseded the founder himself. They were particularly concerned with the use of the brand name and trademark as well as with the social responsibilities of the corporation. In particular, the family office had always been actively involved in a close relationship with the employee representatives. For many years, the company had been spared from severe industrial actions.

The family office had the possibility to appoint several board members due to their significant shareholding and subsequent voting rights at the shareholders meeting. The board member appointed by this owner was called the 'Owner Liaison Director'. He had access to the secretarial services of the PDG and had the right to a work place in the head office building in a room adjacent to the PDG own room.

During the interview with the chairman and CEO, I asked if there was ever any risk of a conflict of interest when he met to discuss strategic issues and thus shared information with the liaison director. He replied:

> No, there is no conflict at all. On the contrary, the director is a real expert in our industry and has excellent connections to suppliers, customers and even competitors. I think we complement each other extremely well. His role is more to act as an advisor to me in matters of strategy related to developments in our industry, regulations, etc. We sometimes go together to meet with legislators and experts at the EU Commission in Brussels. The fact that he has declared his association with the largest owner helps a lot. But of course we share all our conclusions and plans with the rest of the board.

The 'owners' forum

In a UK company that had recently been listed on the London Stock Exchange, the chairman and the board were faced with a small group of institutional investors. These banks and investment funds had been active in the IPO process and invested on behalf of their customers through fiduciary investment arrangements. There were simply no large private shareholders.

The chairman and the CEO had called a meeting with representatives or the large- owner institutions and expressed their concerns about the lack of a counterpart for discussions on long-term strategic goals and vision. The investors had answered that this would have to take place through the traditional governance structure of committees and board meetings. They would be responsible for proposing board member candidates for the annual shareholder meeting and work through established governance channels.

However, a little over a year had passed after the successful listing of the company's shares when the investor representatives were called into a meeting by one of the institutions. At the meeting, they were presented with a plan to form what they later on agreed to call, the 'Owners' Forum'. The five large institutions, all of them UK based, dedicated one person to participate in the meetings of the group.

The Owners' Forum met four times per year, typically ahead of the quarterly reports. They spent one hour discussing various strategic and capital market related issues, before they invited the Chairman as well as the CEO of the company to join them for a brief on status of the company. At their first meeting of the year, they discussed the long-term strategic and financial goals. This served as an input to the Chairman and CEO for the upcoming strategy meeting of the board.

The last meeting of the year was devoted to issues on performance evaluation and principles for compensation. Again, the chairman took part in these discussions together with one other representative from the Compensation Committee.

Over the three years that the Owners' Forum had been in place, the agenda for the meetings became more and more focused on long-term strategy and issues. It was clear to the Chairman and the rest of the board that the forum was an informal gatherings and that no decisions were made or any form of veto was used for decisions otherwise made by shareholders or the board.

When I discussed the experience of the Forum with the chairman, he said the following:

> You see, this is really good! If this group had not existed, who should I have turned to? Maybe I could go to one or two of them. But my experience from doing so in other companies is not very good. It becomes an ad hoc process, and no real issues are ever discussed or penetrated enough. Here we get a good idea of what direction and ambitions the owners have. Normally institutions tend to care for very little than the financial performance of the business. I use to call them the spread-sheet people. But the Forum

discussions and dialogue go beyond the numbers. We discuss real long term strategic issues and how these impact on the corporation. Yes, they have a slight bias towards the capital market and the financial side of things, but that is OK: I report back to the board what we have discussed and it is of great value for all of us at the board. I want to keep it and plan to propose a similar process for another company where I serve as a non-executive director.

The owner representative

In recent years, institutional owners have started to appoint one investment manager to become an 'Owner Representative'. This person does not need to be a member of the board, but has a defined mandate to represent the institutional owner and investor in the interaction with the corporation through the board and its executive management team. The Owner Representative is also responsible for making policy-related decisions on behalf of the institution when required. He/she is backed up by the investment management team dedicated for the specific investment/shareholding in question.

The CEO quarterly report to owners

In some corporations, the CEO has structured a specific process for interacting with the owner(s) or their representatives. This is at least the case for many listed companies. There, the CEO, in the presence of the Chairman in most cases, presents the quarterly report to and answers questions from larger shareholders. This quarterly event is often open also for media representatives and the presentation is typically published on the corporate website on the same day for everyone to see.

This is a direct communication channel between management and the owner. It is important that the board is aware of the various discussions that take place and that the CEO and his/her team is not making special commitments or make specific promises to the owner's representatives. In most cases, meetings follow more routine like procedures and are more of an information exercise.

Board and owner interaction: principles for a Modus Vivendi

This chapter illustrates one of the core themes of corporate governance is the relationship and interaction between the board and the owner. This is an often overlooked dimension of decision-making and strategic management. Yet, this relationship must exist and be actively designed and managed.

Even in the case of an anonymous shareholder, like the absent owner previously mentioned, there should be channels for interaction and communication between the owner and the board. As shown by the preceding experiences, there are several ways of designing a Modus Vivendi for the relationship and interaction.

Another key imperative for the owner and board relationship is to ensure that the owner's perspectives and goals are integrated into the strategic decision-making and corporate governance processes of the corporation. The following elaborates on these issues one by one.

Establishing a modus vivendi for owner and board

First. Let us state as a guiding principle that the relationship between the owner and the board is one of the key dimensions of corporate governance. However, it is often overlooked and sometimes even disregarded.

The experience from having established the different 'meeting places' for owner and board interaction that are described in this chapter has been overwhelmingly positive. It is not the purpose of my work to select and recommend one out of the many versions that exist and were studied. But there must be agreement that there is an imperative need for such an interactive and positive relationship between the owner and the board. This recognition is a major step forward for many corporations.

As previously stated, the most common solution is to appoint the Chairman to be responsible for interacting with the owner(s). The Chairman has been selected to act as the 'liaison' between the owner(s) and the board. In addition to his/her other duties as chairman, this could prove to be a heavy workload requirement and must be carefully considered, especially if the task is to be performed to its full potential.

It seems that other more comprehensive solutions have often proven to be more effective and preferred for corporate governance purposes. We analysed some of these designs in the preceding discussions.

Whether the solution is a form of TROIKA, a 'Presidium', as a 'Strategy Committee' or through similar arrangements, the conclusion is that such a forum should be designed to form part of the recognized corporate governance structure. Therefore, let us explore the lessons learned from examples of 'best practice' that should be implemented by more companies today.

The occurrence of small subsets of board members involving either the owner direct or through a dedicated representative, shows that many corporations are establishing formal governance structures to accommodate the combined involvement from owner, board and management. The examples identified in this book, and there are many others, may work as alternative models for corporate boards and executives to study and learn from. The are two lessons that could also be learned, and thus situations to be avoided, from the corporations I studied:

- Do not create a 'board-in-the-board', that is, avoid fostering an elite 'clique' with huge information and decision-making advantages that could possibly endanger the existing corporate governance structure and processes.

The owner and the board

- Avoid 'board bypassing', that is, where the executive management and/or the CEO establishes direct communication channels with the Owner(s), thereby bypassing the Board and the Chairman.

Translating owner's goals and vision into corporate strategy

The imperative of incorporating the owner's vision and goals into the strategic decision-making process of the corporation has been stated many times throughout this book. I note that this works quite well in family-owned as well as in state-owned companies. The reason is simple; there is a clearly defined and identified owner. And, this owner has a declared interest in having an active role in the strategy formulation and goal-setting process. The situation in a corporation where ownership is more anonymous or at least indirect is different.

We have discussed various governance models aiming at incorporating the owner(s) or his/their representative in the decision-making and governance processes. In practice, it could prove to be difficult to accomplish. However, one Swiss biotech group had developed an interesting approach to this:

> I came onboard to replace the former chairman who was a family member of the largest owner. I adapted an approach to strategic planning that I had sued in other companies in the past. I invited representatives for the two largest owners to join the board for a half day strategy session. Based on the initial discussion on today's situation and strategic options available to the company, the board asked the owner to formulate a set of overall strategic guidelines for the next ten years. For example, we wanted to learn if their key goal was growth or whether a steady and high financial return was the overriding objective. We then used the input from the owners to discuss impact on growth, new R&D initiatives and other strategic initiatives

going forward. The end result was to review the existing strategic plan in the light of these guidelines. Since then we have repeated the process several times. We have even named it the Polaris Plan.

This is indeed a procedure that could be used in most corporations. But the starting point must be to identify and communicate with the owner(s). Thus, we are back to the Modus Vivendi issues as previously outlined. Several examples in my research showed that it works, albeit it requires proactive involvement of both the board and the owner. The Chairman has a clear role to play in this context.

The lack of long-term guidance for the board and subsequently for the executive management team where the owner's vision and goals are being incorporated in the strategy processes is imperative for long-term success of the business. If the owner has no influence or say in the strategy formulation process, it is highly likely that this may cause conflicts and disagreements in the future.

Aligning the owners: setting the shareholder meeting agenda

We have discussed the Modus Vivendi with an owner who has, at least on paper, sufficient controlling interest in the corporation, so that he/they could and should have a say in the strategy process. This has worked in several of the companies I have met during this research as well as in other capacities in the past.

Most publicly listed corporations have a larger group of smaller shareholders. What many times is referred to in capital market jargon as the 'free float'. These are the small shareholders who do not possess more than a few basis points of ownership or less.

In some countries, notably in Germany and in the United States, the corporate law and rules for corporate governance stipulates procedures whereby the smaller shareholders get at least a chance to raise concerns and get additional information. In Germany, the shareholders have the right to register issues and questions to the board (both the Supervisory and Management Boards) at the Annual Meeting. The process is quite formal and time consuming. However, it hardly leads to any direct follow-up discussions or has any impact on the strategy processes of the company. Instead, it serves a purpose of adding transparency and democracy to the entire governance process.

A similar procedure is often found to take place in large US corporations. Issues and questions are often prepared and submitted in advance, so any answers provided by the board at the AGM is typically well prepared and (many times) rehearsed. Other countries have similar or other procedures for the alignment, and sometimes, protection of the small and the minority shareholder. In Chapter 10 on the Board Agenda, I propose that strategic issues should be given a more prominent role on the agenda for the meeting. In fact, I suggest that the board should consider changing the priority and order of the items on the agenda so that strategic issues and initiatives, plus decisions, are given the right focus and attention. This is achieved by placing 'Other Items' on the top of the agenda.

It is particularly important for the board to align the shareholders with the values and goals driving the corporation. It must make a real effort to describe and explain these core themes to the owners. Far too often such key themes are being included somewhere in the Annual report and on the corporate website. Often a lot of effort and hard thinking has gone into the writing of such mission and value statements, so they should also be communicated and understood by the owner. At the same time, the owner must be given a chance to participate in the definition of mission and value statements. These statements cannot just be 'empty words' or words without a strong and joint commitment to them from the owner and the board together.

In many countries, the standard agenda for the AGM is also allocating strategy issues to a limited time typically at the very end of the meeting. Many times, this consists of a long

Powerpoint presentation by the CEO sometimes complemented by the chairman. But it is not aimed at involving the shareholders in the strategy process.

I am convinced that with modern technology, social media resources and skills, corporations can do more in order to enhance the involvement of the shareholders in sharing the long-term strategic issues facing the company. There are many issues at play here, but the goal should be to address this issue for the future.

Visible owner: visible board

I reacted particularly strong to the notion of the absent owner previously mentioned by one of the chairmen. The debate about the lack of direct and active ownership is not new. It points at the need for a shareholder or owner 'Voice'.

A recent example of this debate is the 'Shareholders Rights Project', conducted at Harvard Law School by Professor Lucian Bebchuk. It is an example of where shareholders in corporations with mostly institutional owners could have an influence on the composition and governance model of the board. The proposals urge companies with a staggered board, which allow shareholders to replace only a few directors each year, to place all board members up for election every year. Such a move to regular annual board member elections is aimed at increasing the owner's impact on the board. By enabling shareholders to register their views on all directors each year, the aim is to make boards more accountable to shareholders.

Giving owners more rights to affect the composition and Modus Operandi of the board is not the key issue. Rather, the research has pointed at the need for owners to become more visible to 'show their face'.

In a previous example, we learned about the 'Owner Liaison Director'. It could be argued that there should be a need for a group of institutional owners to appoint an 'Owner Liaison

Officer', meaning that they would select a representative for all of them who is given the mandate to act and speak on behalf of the owners. This role could be circulated between the investors after a given schedule, or simply given to the largest shareholder amongst them, a 'Lead Shareholder'.

'Rejuvenate' the role of the owner

Many of the chairmen and senior board members I spoke to were concerned about the issues related to the involvement of the owner in the corporate governance processes. It is not the purpose of his book to elaborate on all of the ideas and suggestions that were discussed during my research. However, this is a key issue and albeit lots of work has been and is still being done in the area, nevertheless it should be an area for continued research.

The focus should not only lie on the structural issues of corporate governance, but more on the actual involvement of the owner in the core processes that eventually will create value for the corporation and thus for the owners themselves. This involves getting involved in an active dialogue and relationship with the board.

This chapter finishes with an interesting example from an interview with the deputy Chairman of a Japanese industrial conglomerate:

> We regularly invite representatives of the owners to come to special meetings between them and the board. We agree on an agenda where the owners' representatives will first listen to each of the board members and his or her view on strategy of the company and the key issues going forward. Then each owner representative is asked to formulate their specific goals for our business going forward.

> We also spend a lot of time discussing our core values and long term goals. For example, this year we formed a joint

task force consisting of three board member and two owner representatives to work on a specific program to deal with a comprehensive program for our corporate social responsibility. Yes it was influenced by the disaster at the Fukushima nuclear plant and events in the wake of this event, but the idea had been in the process of implementation long before the tragic accident took place last year. This is a new and highly appreciated role for the owners. They and we at the board are very satisfied with the initiative and we plan to enlarge the scope of this group. We call it the 'Joint Values Committee'.

Reality case

Lundin Petroleum: disagreement with owners

Lundin Petroleum (LP) is a Swiss-based oil exploration corporation. It is a publicly listed company, but is still controlled by its largest shareholder, the Lundin family. Lundin Petroleum was funded by the Swedish entrepreneur Adolf Lundin in 1981 originally as International Petroleum, then International Petroleum Corporation, followed by Lundin Oil in the late 1990s. After a series of mergers and acquisitions, in 2001, the company was emerging as Lundin Petroleum. It is listed at the Nasdaq OMX Nordic exchange (LUPE) as well as on the Toronto Stock Exchange (LUP).

Today, LP has proven and probable reserves of 211 million barrels of oil.

In the beginning of its existence, Lundin Oil and Petroleum had a significant interest in oil production in several African countries, including Sudan. Operations in Sudan ceased in 2003. This involvement has led to interest among media especially in Sweden, including the publishing of severe criticism of the company for its actions during this time period.

It resulted in an initiative in March, 2012, where several of the larger institutional owners of LP requested the launch of an independent review of the events in Sudan. At the time, a Swedish prosecutor had already initiated an official investigation into the actions taken by LP in the years in question.

The board and management of LP have opposed the new independent investigation, but have declared that it supports the ongoing official ditto carried out by the Swedish court. In recent events leading up to the Annual Shareholders Meeting in May 2012, the CEO of LP publicly expressed his dissatisfaction with the proposed independent investigation.

The proposal for the independent review has been publicly supported by some of the large institutional investors in LP. One of the larger institutional owners, the Folksam Group, recently said, 'Our proposal (to investigate the matter in a separate analysis; my comment) stands firm. It is now up to the general meeting to decide on the matter. We are awaiting the outcome of any vote at the meeting,' says a representative for this owner.

Recently, the LP CEO went as far as to suggest that owners who were supporting the proposal should sell their shares instead.

> We want to have a solid group with long term institutional investors, but if institutions and other shareholders do not trust the management and board, they should sell their shares. Everybody knows tat the management and board do not support an investigation, and there are several institutional owners who are also against such an initiative.

He goes on to add:

> During recent years, the share of international investors has increased in the company. This group of owners does not want an investigation and is surprised that this proposal has been raised. They have a longer experience of investing in natural resource based industries and in emerging markets. ... The shareholders must trust the management team and allow the ongoing public court investigation to proceed. It is time to look ahead and not go backwards.

It should be noted that the Lundin family controls over one-third of the total number of shares. Swedish retail shareholders account for only 11 per cent of the total.

The board is headed by Ian Lundin, Chairman of Lundin Petroleum, and son of Adolf Lundin, the Founder.

Lessons to be learned

Reality case: 'Lundin Petroleum'

- The issue has not been subject to a joint discussion between the board and some of the major institutional owners.
- This has led to a locked situation and the process has also been displayed in media where both sides communicate openly through the press.
- It is an example of how a relationship between key owners and the board should not be designed and managed.

CHAPTER 6
The one team board challenge

Introduction: the 'one team' board

In the ideal world, where we could start by building the board on a 'blank sheet of paper', we would naturally focus on how to build a board where the directors complement each other, and how their combined skills could play together to the benefit of the corporation they are set to serve. If we were free to design and find the optimal board team, we would be looking to a set of imperatives when making the selections:

- We would appoint members who complement each other and who bring key skills and expertise to the board and enhance quality and accuracy of decision-making. Cultural and gender diversity should also be part of the profile definition.
- We must make everyone understand that they all serve the interest of the company; they are not selected to look after self-interests, be part of power struggles between shareholder factions, involve themselves in politicking, lobbying and so on. They also must be committed to give the CEO and his team full support.
- At all cost we must avoid involving members who cannot listen and/or who like to listen only to themselves. This is a personality issue and not so much a matter of expertise and track record (even though they, not surprisingly, tend to be related), but it is a key factor for board performance.
- Finally, in an existing board structure, it is ultimately the task of the chairman to promote the One Team spirit and

modus operandi. By setting the standards and following up on individual board member performance, the chairman can actively promote and build a board consisting of team players who set the company's interests first and their own aspirations and objectives later.

The challenge

Why is the One Team Board very rarely a reality in almost any corporation, regardless of ownership structure? In fact, many times the boards of publicly traded company show less of the One Team nature than boards in family office groups, not for profit organizations, or even state-owned corporations. Why is this so? Why do boards tend to underperform the true combined potential of their members?

There are many reasons for this, of course. Let us turn to some of the more relevant:

- One cause for the board's inability to perform to its potential is easy to define; the simple lack of common values and goals. Many boards do not act as a team simply because the members are not aware of where the corporation is or should be going. They cannot unite under one 'banner', as they do not understand what the end result should be. This issue could be resolved through the structured approach to the *modus operandi* of the board.
- Another reason is more complex in nature and harder to deal with. In many corporations, especially in listed companies, the board consists of representatives for the various shareholder groups; often representing institutional investors or strategic investors. This has sometimes led to rivalries and even open conflicts between such differing parties pursuing their own 'agendas' and objectives for the business and their own investments and holdings.
- The use of a specifically assigned Nominating Committee offers certain advantages, but, as we have seen in the

research, could also bring even worse disorder to the governance system. This Nominating Committee must not be the instrument through which individual shareholders or groups thereof can manipulate the selection of board members, to be those who would support their own agendas; to become 'a battleground in the battleground'. This has been observed in many cases where institutional shareholders, banks and other stakeholders utilize the Nominating Committee solely for their own purposes and goals. This must be avoided at all costs.
- The board might lack clear and robust leadership; the chairman could be a 'lame duck' or simply not doing his/her job adequately. As a result, the board members are not acting as One Team and there is nobody in charge of correcting this situation.
- In some well-known cases, the board has also been 'hijacked' by a (too) powerful CEO and his management team; in the worst case, this could also happen when the chairman and the CEO is the one and same person. We have seen disastrous examples of where the board has simply been led into making decisions entirely manipulated by the 'hijacker' to serve whatever purpose they happen to be pursuing. A 'hijacker' has also in some cases been the egocentric board member who uses the board meetings as their personal 'ego booster', a true recipe for disaster.
- Another reason why the team is not acting as a One Team is when the skill profiles are too similar or not complementary at all. Either the team lacks some critical core competencies, or the directors are simply too similar in background, experience, management skills, strategic thinking and cultural base.
- This could also be the case when there is a lack of diversity among board members, whether it is industry, previous experience, or gender. The latter is a focus of a lot of debate in many countries, at supranational levels, and not least in media and the public.
- Finally, the too large size of the board could prevent a One Team to evolve. Some boards consist of too many board

members. In some cases, I found examples of boards that consisted of over thirteen people. It is very hard, if not impossible, to create the kind of One Team spirit that we are looking for in such large groups.

Let us turn to each of these in the following sections.

Lack of common vision and goals

The research revealed the anecdote of a chairman who met together with his board at a one day Strategy Retreat, the purpose of the event was partly to strengthen the board as a group, or 'Team Building' as the chairman called it in his letter before the meeting. They never got further than the first item on the agenda, before the entire group became engaged in a fierce debate about the very *raison d'être* for the business; that is, 'What are we really doing and what should we be doing?' They clearly stated that as board members they had very poor knowledge about goals and strategy of the company, including such fundamental issues such as 'What business are we really in?', 'What justifies our existence?' and so on. After two days of intense discussions about fundamentals of vision and strategy, the meeting concluded with at least a general perspective on overall direction. Afterwards the chairman confided:

> We needed this exercise; this is actually the first time we have ever discussed these key issues for the company; we must all have taken for granted our mission and justification for what we do and why we exist. But better now than never.

A scaring experience, but eventually very useful. Whether or not as a result of this exercise (where the CEO and the CFO also participated), the company's stock did rise in value with over 120 per cent over the next twelve months (beating the market by at least ten times).

Power struggles at board level

The governance system as defined by corporate law, in most jurisdictions, is designed to allow the shareholders to exercise their influence both through shareholder votes as well as by appointing directors to the board. Even if most corporate legislation gives shareholders the right to assign board seats to directors based on straightforward voting rules, in reality the final composition of the board is often formed as a result of agreements between various shareholders and groups of these. When so appointed, board members are obliged to act on behalf of all shareholders in the corporation and on what is deemed the best for the business overall. Not to act in order to safeguard the interests and objectives of just one single shareholder or group.

In the study, many examples were found where such vested interests tended to guide and determine both the *modus operandi* of the board (in negative ways) as well as to create a vast bias in their decision-making and general behaviour as board members.

Such power struggles could create large problems for the board and there are several examples where the board, as a result, has become a 'battlefield' where various power struggles tend to overshadow the real issues and lead to serious sub-optimization and even to wrong decisions with very negative consequences for the board as a whole. Rather than enjoying a 'we-we-we' approach to the challenges of the corporation, the goal of protecting what was regarded as the best solution for its own interests resulted in a 'me first and only' syndrome. No teamwork was ever allowed to evolve and the board stopped acting as an effective body for both governance and strategic guidance of the corporation. It simply became an instrument for negative value creation.

The challenge is clear, but the vision of putting the 'Dream Team' together in one single corporate board can unfortunately remain just another dream. The potential breeding ground for power struggles will always exist, almost regardless of how well-structured and systematic the selection and retention processes for the board members are designed. As long as ownership is spread among different shareholders and their respective groups, there will always be separate agendas and goals.

In a family-owned business the situation is different. Here the challenge is of a different sort: to optimize the skills and value creation potential of the board, for the board members to define their roles so as to both serve the corporation and its shareholder(s), and at the same time maintain a high level of integrity and keep the interest of the business at a high standard.

Finally, as can be seen in many countries, state-owned companies tend to assign different roles for the board members. Often, these represent varying stakeholder interests, such as political parties and movements, regional interests and tend to be driven by non economic value goals.

Wrong role of the nominating committee

The problem of assembling the best possible team for the board is not unknown to most companies. Many attempts have been made to deal with ways of putting together a good and working team for the board.

One way of dealing with the selection and composition issues is when the board members are recruited and proposed by the Nominating Committee; this is a good system, as it should, at least in theory, allow directors to be nominated and elected based on skills and potential contribution to the business of the corporation. However, in the study, we observed several situations where the real problem did not arise in the actual selection procedure, but rather in the appointment of the committee members. In some cases, they became the 'extended arm' of the various groups of shareholders with the potential to manipulate the composition of the board.

The alternative is to go back to the original idea behind regulation of the corporate governance, that is, to allow shareholders to vote at the General Meeting. The Nominating Committee structure is a way to facilitate this otherwise very complex and often cumbersome process. Finally, to allow the chairman with or without the consensus of the other board members to both nominate and elect a director is the least attractive of the options at hand.

One chairman, who was very happy with the way her board had been assembled, put it this way:

> We approach the selection and engagement of new board members just as we would hire key managers for the firm; we engage outside counsel for the selection process. We establish profiles for the 'optimal' profile of a new board member, and then ask the advisor to search for a suitable candidate. The ultimate choice is both screened and proposed by the nominating committee, but only after the proposed candidate has been effectively vetted by both the existing board members and the key shareholder groups.... I have a lot of say in this decision making process, as I put more emphasis on the team building side, and how the new member could add to the value creation potential of this board through valuable experience or skills that he/she could offer to the existing team; we call it 'team synergies' in our company.

In a family-owned business, the situation is different. Here the challenge is of a different sort: to optimize the skills and value creation potential of the board, for the board members to define their roles so as to both serve the corporation and its shareholder(s), to maintain a high level of integrity, and keep the interest of the business at high standards.

Lack of leadership

Regardless of how the chairman decides to define the role they are taking on, there is clearly one role where they must perform – the role as the leader of the team that constitutes the board. 'I take a very active role in team-building', said one chairman interviewed. He added:

> Every year I organize an activity or event outside of the regular board curriculum, aimed at gathering momentum for our team, and to build the 'team spirit'. This is highly appreciated among my fellow board members, and we try to arrange the events to be as open and socially oriented as possible. Last year we all went trekking in the mountains, for example. We stayed overnight in tents and cooked dinner over open fireplaces. Every evening we had defined a common theme for discussion; a theme that related to the way we work together and how we could use each board members strengths to his or her best advantage. This event and other similar in the past have really contributed to boost our team spirit and we work so much better and harder than before. And we have lots of fun together at the same time. I hope other boards do the same as we do.

Clearly, the chairman has a leadership role to play that goes beyond the chairing of the actual board meetings, setting the agenda, and interacting with the CEO. The task of leadership for the board team members is hard to define, and there is no clear reporting relationship such as in a typical managerial structure. Rather, the chairman must define their own 'rules of engagement' and try out the best possible approach for the board in question.

Another chairman shared her experience:

> I spend at least one long meeting per year with each board member, one by one, to discuss this particular member's performance and strengths and weaknesses. And how we could work together at the board to leverage those specific skills and potential contribution to the extent possible; we define the specific tasks that this board member should perform in addition to the normal director duties. We also

try to evaluate the performance and specific contributions to the corporation through his/her board membership. And we set specific goals and define key initiatives for him/her going forward. It really pays off, and I could then follow up over time and make necessary improvements and correct any major deviations from the agreed plan. And all the board members truly appreciate this interaction and the feedback I give them.

Board hijacking

This specific problem has been observed during the research in several cases. The term 'Hijacking' was used by one chairman who had just left one chair position because of the perceived impossible situation he faced with a CEO who had imposed himself on the board, by positioning information with the board in a way that influenced their ability to analyse and prioritize between proposals. The chairman described the situation as follows for me:

> We [the board members] were presented with information that he [the CEO] had manipulated for his own agenda and purposes; we had no chance but to use it and try to understand whether it was real data or just bits and pieces of the reality behind the issues at stake. A terrifying experience... Eventually we tried to do some vetting with the use of the CFO, but he was too close to the CEO, and hence left us with even more doubts about what was really going on in the company. We at the board were being 'hijacked' by the CEO and his team. I decided to leave my position and brought the entire story up at the General Meeting; but no one seemed to care. Now a new chairman has come on-board and I can only wish him the best of luck; I tried my best but in vain.

One chairman interviewed was extremely infuriated because of the egocentric behaviour of one of his directors. Obviously the board member in this case was deliberately using the board as a place to exercise his own (hidden) agenda and made most board meetings less effective than they should be. The chairman said:

> This particular director is abusing the board to boost his own ego. He is challenging documents, is asking for third party reviews such as lawyers, accountants, and consultants all the time. Nothing wrong with this per se, but he does it on purpose, as a means to distract the other board members. I have tried to get rid of him, but he is close to the largest owner and I have not been successful so far. It is a real shame and costs us lots of valuable time.

Lack of key skills and core competencies

As emphasized by many scholars, the selection of board members should be based on what skills and competencies the corporation need. Depending on the industry structure, the challenges ahead, specific need for support, and so on, the board members should be selected with the best interest and needs of the company in mind. Again, a professionally composed Nominating Committee should be able to define such profiles and conduct a search and recruitment process aligned to find the best possible candidates for the job. This process must avoid a system where the 'Old Boys Club' criteria become the overwhelming guidance for this selection process. There are far too many so called 'Board Professionals', members of the 'Old Boys Club', who sit on each other's boards, and never contribute to the value creation for the company they should serve.

Lack of diversity

A lot of discussion has been held on the need for diversity of board members, particularly as for gender diversity. We have seen the request for legislation and even quotas for board membership for publicly listed companies, where this has even taken place in some countries such as Norway.

The need for diversity was discussed during most of the research interviews with the board chairmen. Out of the sample of thirty-eight chairmen, only four were women, which may bias the findings. However, ten per cent of female chair persons is higher than the prevailing average for most countries, and even exceeds total female board membership percentage in most cases.

Boards are too large

The boards are many times too large. In the research we found, corporations where boards consisted of up to fifteen directors. It is simply too many. It becomes too difficult to keep a focus on key strategic issues. Everybody wants to have a say during the discussions leading us to a decision or vote. The fact that the size of the board is growing rather than decreasing seems to be a trend in many markets today, for example, in some Scandinavian countries.

Here a lot could be learned from Private Equity, where boards are used as a key tool for both strategy formulation and implementation. A portfolio company board in a Private equity group typically consists of four to six members. The larger the size of the board, the less initiative is left for the individual board member. I am strongly in favour of smaller boards, even in large corporate groups. No board should be larger than ten directors as a rule of thumb. This view was confirmed by most of the chairmen and senior board members I interviewed during the research.

To summarize the view of most of the interviewees, the following could be concluded on the issue of gender diversity:

1. The key selection criteria for board members should be how well their core competencies and skills match the needs of the specific company in question.

2. The general experience of increasing the number of women at board level has been overwhelmingly positive. As one chairman (a male) observed: 'We have three women on the board now out of a total of nine board members, an increase by two during the last couple of years. I find that the entire process for discussions, analysis, and decision-making, has improved significantly with the addition of women to the board. They add a degree of seriousness to the decision-making and especially the preparation process. I dare say that our board is working much better now than before when we had less than ten per cent of women on the board... I would not mind increasing the proportion of female board members even more. They have impacted our entire operation for the better. We are more focused and better prepared than before. Thanks to them I am sure.'
3. But the way to go forward should not be through quotas. Instead, more emphasis should be on training potential board member candidates to do a better job once elected. To encourage more executives, both men and women, to improve the skills required to be able to serve at a board and create value to the corporation. Such programs could be marketed especially to women, such as using social media networks to reach out to, and to increase the general interest for and attractiveness of becoming a board member in general, and for women in particular.
4. Once women come on as board members, they often have had a very positive impact (the chairman previously quoted was not alone at all in having positive views on increasing female board representation). Encourage business schools and executive education providers to offer more programs aimed for potential board members.

Summary and recommendations

The topics covered in this article are broad and complex in nature. But we should keep it simple and also, to some extent, be humble about how to try to resolve them.

The one team board challenge

The starting point for most of the chairmen interviewed is that the board must be given a more important and relevant role for the corporations they serve, so that they can create real value for the businesses and organizations, support the CEO and their team with strategy formulation and implementation, and act as a professional governance body for the shareholders.

Here are some key recommendations for how to create a 'One Team Board':

- Select board members based on the company's specific need for core competencies and skills, not on friendship, or, even worse, from the 'Old Boys Club'. Define key profiles for the new board member selection process.
- Do not allow individual shareholder groups to capture the board and use it as a 'battleground' for their own agendas and goals.
- Select a Nominating Committee that is not biased and in itself consists of members with various backgrounds and skills; avoid the 'battleground within the battleground' at all costs.
- Allow the Nominating Committee to design a professional selection and recruiting process for new board members, similar to hiring a senior executive for the corporation.
- The chairman must act as the Team Leader and work hard to create teamwork and alignment around the overall goals and targets of the corporation.
- The chairman must also act decisively and fast to deal with individual board members who either abuse the board process, or use it for their own personal aspirations and 'games'; better to ask a board member to leave in time, than wait until further damage has been done.
- Diversity should be encouraged as long as its serves the overall interest of the company and adds to the value creation potential of the board as a One Team. Increasing the number for women on boards has shown many positive effects in the examples studied in this research. Today,

women often have to have an exceptional skill set because of the fact that boards are predominantly male. In the end of the day, women and men should be chosen as board members on equal terms, with the same requirements of professional skills and core competencies.
- Quotas should be avoided. Instead, we must encourage executives to become board members, and provide incentives to business schools and talent developers to offer training programs for potential board members. These programs to need to be marketed to women in order to prepare them for and increase their willingness and preparedness to serve as board members in the future. Over time, this would lead to a process where natural selection takes over from formal and bureaucratic structures and systems.

If this could lead to more value creating boards, we have achieved a lot. Hopefully, this contributes significant added value to the development of long-term growth and sustainability for corporations worldwide.

Reality case

The mountain team building experience

A chairman of an industrial group was known for his devotion to outdoor activities. He is a keen fan of trekking, cross country skiing and even mountaineering.

Thus, maybe it is no surprise that once a year he invites the entire board to join him for a full day of activities at a place that he had carefully selected for the purpose of allowing the board to spend time together under very nice conditions.

The group of twelve board members, including the chairman plus the CEO, met the previous night in a hotel in the resort. The CEO had briefed them on the recent strategic initiatives that were being implemented throughout the group. As the company consisted of over seven separate business areas, the

The one team board challenge

review was quite comprehensive. But the CEO had ended the review of each initiative by presenting a set of key issues that he wanted the board to consider for each of the ongoing rollouts.

After the CEO presentation and discussion, the chairman had summarized the various points raised for each of the initiatives. He ended the evening session with, 'Tomorrow during the walk, I want us to spend the morning discussing these issues in small groups. I will go back and forth between the groups and listen and comment. The CEO will meet us at our lunch break.'

They set out from the hotel at seven thirty in the morning. Along the trekking route that took the board members along some narrow and picturesque tracks, they stopped a few times to eat and rest. The chairman had prepared an activity at each stop, where the members were asked to perform various tasks. In fact, it was a form of competition between the smaller groups.

The afternoon was entirely devoted to continued trekking and various stops along the route. One was called 'tir d'arc', that is, shooting with a bow and arrow on a board. The chairman was the referee but could not resist shooting a few arrows himself.

At the second stop, the groups were asked to paddle a canoe in teams of four across a small lake. As the canoes were narrow and small, this required a good sense of teamwork from each crew. Again, the crossing was declared to be a race by the chairman whereas the arrival positions of the teams were added to the previous arch event.

At lunchtime, each group was asked to present the results from their strategic discussions during the morning walk. The chairman took notes together with the CEO. They did not comment on any of the suggestions and comments from the three groups.

Upon return from the day's activities, the chairman had arranged a barbecue dinner in front of the hotel. He encouraged each group to come forward and present their views on the various strategic initiatives as discussed earlier during the day. They were supported by the CEO, who had documented the previous discussions over lunch.

The result of the discussions and presentations were summarized in a strategy document that was to be circulated among the board members. It was not given to the rest of the management team at this point in time.

Lessons to be learned

Reality case: 'The Team Building Exercise'

- The Chairman should take the initiative to create a spirit of the 'One Team'.
- One Team is achieved through interaction and openness.
- It builds on the fact that each board member adds relevant skills and competence to the One Team.
- Team skills and competencies should be complementary by design.

CHAPTER 7
Leading through times of change and disruption

The board: leader in times of change and disruption

In this book, we focus on many aspects of how the board could and should create value for the corporation it serves. We also focus on how the board itself should be formed and how to design its modus operandi to obtain successful results from its work.

Based on the findings from my research, however, I would argue that the role to act as a leader and catalyst for change, as well as how to proactively lead through the impact of changes the external environment of the company, ranks highest among the key priorities for the board. It is also important that the board offer to share its experience and advice to executive management.

One Chairman in an Amsterdam based financial services company, elaborated on this key issue as follows:

> There are times when management simply does not know what should guide their decisions; they feel uncertain about the future and want to get guidance in terms of how careful we should be, now much of a safety net the company should create in the case of a prolonged crisis. But there are also issues the top team does not want to bring to the attention of the entire board for decision or even worse, without having come to a proper resolution between

themselves on direction and magnitude of changes that lie ahead.

We understand this and have arranged for a smell subset of the board to act as a group of senior advisors to the management team. They could be called a couple of times per year or, in the case of an emergency or a crisis coming up, with very short notice.

The CEO feels no obligation to do so, and the members are very keen to offer their advice based on their own experience. It is informal and no formal agenda exists nor are any minutes taken.

Thus, a key role of the board in most corporations is related to its ability to support management and the organization to understand the need for managing and implementing change. Of great importance is also how to proactively react to change implemented by others, by competitors, new entrants, overall business cycles and other relevant external factors. Thus, the issue is how the board could and should act both proactively to grow the business of the company and also to react to changes in its external environment. Finally, the board must be able to correct management when it has embarked on a strategic route and direction that, if not stopped or changed, most likely will cause severe problems for the corporation. This chapter is devoted to the role of the board in such change related actions and initiatives.

Let us start with the situations where the board should be a catalyst for strategic change in the company. First, this is the case where the board should take a proactive role in dealing with reluctance or resistance to change on behalf of management.

This is the case of a need to change the existing strategy because of strategic underperformance. It must not go as far as the entire society of Easter Island or the Mayas, but the failure to acknowledge that the chosen strategy and direction of the company is not going to achieve the potential of the business, or even lead to long-term failure of the company, is bad enough. Like a CEO who is quoted later in this chapter

Leading through times of change and disruption

says, '... but this is the way we always have done things...'. Meaning, 'why change?'.

The board must not accept a strategic status quo just because the performance right now is 'good enough'. This kind of acceptance of 'satisfactory underperformance' has been disastrous for many companies in the past. Second, the board must push management and the organization on innovation and creating new business models. This was discussed in a separate section of this book (Chapter 8).

There are four situations where the board should be leading the company in its efforts to deal with change and disruption coming from external factors. We look at these in the following paragraphs, but in summary they are: the impact of business cycles on the business dynamics of the company, how the business is faced with the unexpected, the 'Black Swans' and how the board must act to get rid of the 'Holy Cows' of the business and the 'eternal truths' that most organizations are full of. Finally, we take a look at how the board acts as advisors to the management team in line with what the Dutch chairman previously stated about ? For example, forming smaller teams of board members that are acting as informal advisors to the management team.

Leading for change

The CEO of a large global white goods group once said the following about change:

> In addition to the Ten Commands, we have two more; 'this is the way we always have done things' and 'we have never done it this way before'. These are two extra commands and rules that effectively stop all change work in a corporation.

This is a very true statement. We have seen many examples of corporations that have refused to change or simply have not realized the need to change. The ever existing 'resistance to change' is also a key factor that explains why many companies, albeit possessing extraordinary skills in anticipating and evaluating change, simply fail to leverage from such insights that would otherwise have enabled them to benefit from 'first mover advantages' and other disruptive moves.

In the section on Board and Innovation (Chapter 8), we discussed the nature and impact of new business models and innovation as well as how the board could act to encourage and push for such new ideas and subsequent change. Today, nobody would argue that innovation is not the single most important driver of long-term sustainable growth and profitability. To continuously look for proactive change has become a guiding principle, a 'mantra, for most companies aspiring to reach world class levels of performance'.

As we see throughout this chapter, sometimes change is required even in a business that is doing seemingly well in its industry. The previous quote is a clear indication of this. There are two dimensions of why change needs to be managed even in a business that on paper is performing relatively well. This aspect of performance management is discussed in Chapter 9, Board and Boosting Peak Performance.

It is worth emphasizing that many times such performance is not even close to the full potential of the business. Unfortunately, it is often the case that 'good enough' is to allow management to continue on its chosen track. This is often the case for financial underperformance, because strategic underperformance is harder to observe and grasp.

One Chairman of a US-based technology company told me:

> We were the market leader in a well- defined segment of the market where the business had operated for over twenty years. This was the initial market entry point for the company and we had developed the business well therein. It was just that the adjacent segments were growing at rates that sometimes were double that of our segment. Management was not very keen to even consider

entering these new growth areas. They were afraid that such moves might dilute the efforts in what they perceived to be our core business. But the board challenged this 'paradigm'. We engaged a strategy consulting firm to evaluate the attractiveness and proposed strategy for entering the adjacent segments, those beyond the perceived core. We found that the potential size of this new market space was many times bigger than our existing core, and that growth rates were at least double as high.

We asked the management team to elaborate on these findings and then report back to the board with a new strategic plan outlining a possible roll out in these new market segments. We are now in the process of making inroads into the growth areas, both by new product development and adjustments, as well as through an m & a strategy aiming at buying existing competitor in the new areas.

Therefore, one important aspect of the board's role in change management is to act as a catalyst for change from existing perceived core business into new growth areas. This is not against the will of the executive management team, but in a joint initiative to evaluate and possibly change the existing strategic paradigm prevailing in the corporation.

The other side of that equation, however, is how to respond to such new challenges and ideas. Markides (2010) elaborates on how existing competitors could react to new entrants and disruptive solutions to the existing business models. These are issues more related to the enterprise level such as business models, new competitors, innovation and so on.

Learning from the past: acting for the future

The board should and could take a leadership role in promoting and act as a catalyst for change. But it must also lead the company in its efforts to react to changes and disruption in its external environment.

We are all aware of the impact of changes in the economic cycle. Good times that were believed to last forever suddenly go away and leave place for more difficult times. At least, that is what we perceive will happen. To understand and manage business cycles is one of management's key tasks.

What about reacting to the changes that take place more gradually over time? Even worse, how could a board or a management team anticipate changes and disruptions whose impact on the business is huge, yet are almost impossible to predict, especially when it comes to the timing of their occurrence?

The business world and society have witnessed many major disruptions and unexpected changes to the normal dynamics of the environment in which the corporation operates. Every time there is a recession, many companies and boards alike, stand still and seem to be struck by lightning – as if the change from a Bull to a Bear market was something completely unexpected and even unheard of in history.

In the aftermath to the 2008 collapse of the financial markets, some experts even tried to explain the seemingly complete 'surprise effect' observed among many professional managers on Wall Street, in the City of London, Frankfurt, Paris, Hong Kong, Tokyo and in all financial centres in the world. Few, if any, were able not only to predict and foresee the downfall, but also to turn their insights into rational decision-making.

As has been thoroughly described by many authors, such as Michael Lewis in *The Big Short* (Lewis, 2010), *The Greatest Trade Ever*, by Gregory Zuckerman (Zuckerman, 2009), Hank Paulson in *On the Brink* (Paulson, 2010), and Andrew Ross Sorkin in *Too Big to Fail* (Sorkin, 2009), very few, if any, of the key players in the world of finance, were even close to predicting the collapse of the housing bubble with sub-prime loans, securitized debt packages and the use of Credit Default Swaps to proactively benefit from a predicted downturn. Yet, we know from history, that such speculative 'bubbles' will eventually burst.

Leading through times of change and disruption

What had Wall Street really learned from the past? Had Wall Street investment bankers ever heard of or studied, for example, the Tulip Mania in Holland during the seventeenth century? Obviously not, a lot most experts would say. But should they not have learned at least from more recent 'bubbles' and over-speculation such as the Dotcom crash of 2000?

That crash was a huge change in valuations of Internet companies that sent the capital markets and the underlying 'real economy' into a downward spiral. This occurred only eight years before the Lehman Brothers bankruptcy sent the whole world into one of its worst recessions ever.

Is the memory of well-educated and high paid executives so short and fragile? Or is it so that when people act as a crowd, they tend to disregard the obvious and unpleasant facts and hope and pray that no bad news emerges? The latter is probably the case. Other evidence of negligence to the obvious can be found when looking at the collapse of entire societies and cultures because of the unwillingness or ability to face reality, and act accordingly to avoid a disaster or crisis. Scholars have studied the lessons that can be learned from the final collapse of the society on Easter Island. This was a long-term process, but ultimately the collapse was a fact when the last parts of the forest were cut down. Jared Diamond in his work *Collapse* (Diamond, 2005) raises the very relevant question, 'What did the Easter islander who cut down the last palm tree say while he was doing it?'

Other such known examples of collapses caused by seemingly wrong decisions or (from our perspective) irrational behaviour are the collapse of Maya culture. I think there are many lessons that could be learned from such major disruptions, naivety and negligence. One issue could be traced to what some may see as irrational behaviour, whereas in fact it is indeed rational albeit being 'bad' and harmful to others. Another example is, without any doubt, the subprime bubble and its consequences when it finally burst. With hindsight, the enormous expanding of household credits where lending took place to borrowers who even with a fraction of analysis could have been judged to have no or insufficient creditworthiness, that is, the ability to service such debt, was not irrational. Rather, it was a planned outcome of irresponsible but conscious over lending to subprime borrowers by banks and financial institutions who were guided by other goals and values than common business practice.

Leading through change and disruption

The occurrence of business cycles is one aspect of how corporations are being faced with the need to change and adapt to changes in the environment. Pursuing actions leading to the long-term depreciation of key ingredients for long-term sustainability is maybe an extreme version of such inability to accommodate and deter change. There is one major aspect of the role of the board that is sometimes overlooked. It is when the board is faced with an external challenge facing the ongoing modus operandi of the business.

When new rules of engagement are being introduced and the familiar environment suddenly changes, a disruption to what is normal occurs. Chapter 8 discusses how the board should play an active role in promoting and supporting innovation in the organization.

Let us now turn to a set of specific changes and disruptive events in the external environment that have significant impact on the conditions under which the business operates and competes.

The board and cycles

The phenomenon referred to as business cycles is not new to any business person. We all know that they exist, and still we cannot really learn how to predict them coming and going without some margin of error, nor perfect design processes to deal with them.

Leading through times of change and disruption

Many management teams spend lots of time thinking about cycles. Not only in known cyclical industries such as semiconductors, shipping, pulp and paper, steel, construction and so on, but in almost any business and geography today.

Peter Drucker wrote:

> As long as business men focus their thinking on the business cycle they will be dominated by the business-cycle psychology. They will therefore make the wrong decision no matter how good their intentions and how good the economists analytical ability. (Drucker, 1955)

One Chairman told me:

> 'I have been in business since I left university. For over forty years now. First as a young business and general manager, then as a CEO, board member, and now as a chairman. I guess I have been part of at least six or maybe even seven recessions. And I have seen at least three major stock exchange crashes. I know and have learned the hard way that what goes up eventually will go down, and vice versa. From experience, I know that we will hit the bottom of the curve and start getting back up again. Yes, I know this is happening, and still I do not know how I could and should relate this experience to my colleagues at the board level. I am not alone though. At our board, where are a group of grey haired people and we have all been through the same experience of ups and downs. I sometimes ask myself why I do not react more strongly when we plan for an eternal bright future. I hope I will find a good answer before I retire.

During the research, the issue of cycles and their impact on long-term strategic decision-making with most of the board members and executives I met. They did not all share the view of the Chairman previously quoted, but they were all concerned about the impact of cycles and how to deal with this at the board level.

A Chairman in a pharmaceutical company gave this interesting view:

> I know that there will be downturns and then the good times will come back. But in our industry, we cannot allow cyclical dimensions impact on our long term strategic decisions. When we make a decision to invest in a new drug development initiative, this typically represents a minimum of a thirty to fifty year time commitment. From the initiation of research to the expiration of the patents eventually happens. These decisions are what we call cycle-proof.
>
> But then we have defined the 'cycle-exposed' elements of our investment process. Here the board asks management to establish contingency plans for how to manage both investments and expenditures in the case of changing business conditions. It may sound over-simplified to many, and is probably not what they teach students at Harvard Business School, but in our case, it seems to work. At least it puts the focus on what parts of our business is exposed to the cycles and what other parts must be treated as pure long term.

Most companies have a plan in place for how to react to an economic downturn. But it is surprising to find how such short-term plans tend to be put in place without proper analysis of their long-term impact. The obvious cuts always come first: after years of spending on lavish Christmas parties, employee benefits, 'giveaways' to customers, and similar signs of the 'sunny days', when the change comes and the 'rainy days' are back again, we look at empty fruit baskets in the canteen, no free milk for the coffee in the fridges, cancelled celebration events or maybe even the Christmas party has been 'postponed'.

It is one of the core tasks and responsibilities of the executive management team of a corporation to keep track of changes both close to the market space and environment in which the business operates as well as the long-term trends and dynamics of the external environment, both within and external to the industry of the corporation.

The management literature is full of wisdom and theories for how to keep track of changes in the external environment that could impact the business of the company. Some of us still remember the days of long-range planning when management adapted an almost scientific approach to forecasting and planning for the business. They were staffed with budgeting teams and long-range planning departments (these could sometimes be one of or even the largest corporate staff at the Head Office). They were using very sophisticated models with a web of parameters affecting the core elements of the business. Unfortunately, these models had some major drawbacks associated with them; most notably, the fact that the future was always supposed to be a projected continuation of the past and that the future development was mostly linear with very little or none of the cyclical realities of all businesses actually incorporated.

Various forecasting models and tracking systems are still in use to help guide the management team in its decision-making on strategy and operations both in the near to longer- term time scale. There is absolutely nothing wrong with that, on the contrary, the very notion of thinking and planning ahead is a core management process.

Typically, such forecasts and projections influence the planning and budgeting process. If a general positive macroeconomic development is in sight, our own sales are likely to be 'riding the curve' and thus show a generally positive development, if only by following the general upturn in the economy and not by gaining market share or introducing new products and services or increasing prices.

These are the plans and budgets that the board is presented with. It is part of the board's responsibility to challenge the key underlying assumptions that form part of the plans and budgets. This is particularly the case when the board engages in setting the goals and targets for the management team.

Rarely do such opinions of the board lead to anything more than possible revisions and adjustments to the plans. In fact, they should affect the definition of the goals and targets. 'We are happy with the plans that our CEO and his team presents', stated one Chairman. 'But sometimes we need to ask some rather simple questions in order to validate the accuracy of the plans. We do this mostly to avoid being presented by pure 'hockey stick' plans, where everything is going our way and nothing could possibly stop the business from growing. But most of the time the team seems to have considered the external impact on our business conditions.'

An interesting aspect of leading through cycles is told by the founder and CEO of a large international professional service firm:

> We are prepared for downturns; in fact, our most successful strategic moves have occurred when times have been hard in our industry. We are offering a product (executive training, my comment), that is highly sensitive to the macro economic cycles. Our clients are often short sighted when bad times hit, and our services are often some of the first that are cut out. We know that from experience.

He went on to add:

> But we have designed a specific plan for how to benefit from downturns; it is well rehearsed and ready to be launched if and when the bad times come. Typically, most of our competitors react by stopping hiring of new talent, even closing offices and laying of staff. We try to build a reserve for this. In fact, in the last two recessions, we have acquired two complementary businesses and actively pushed client acquisition programs, offering new and enhanced services to new clients where our competitors are cutting back on their customer management efforts. I have discussed this plan with the board and they have approved of this approach. It is now a cornerstone of our corporate strategy.

This proactive approach to cope with the impact of cycles is not unique, but the systematic approach to benefit from changes in the external environment is very interesting. To summarize, the impact of business cycles on our economies has shown up very clearly in recent years. The fact that cycles turn and result in major gain and loss of value and momentum is now something boards and management teams must integrate into their approach to strategy and business in general. In/out, long/short, are no longer buzzwords from the trading rooms of brokers and banks. They have become imperatives for most companies aspiring to successfully compete.

Here the board has a key role to play by using its experience from past changes in the cycles to support and coach senior management in the subsequent change programs. To point out that a 'recipe for success' in a fast growing economy may be a 'fast track' to disaster in another phase of the cycle and vice versa. This means that the board needs to think about the required approach and competencies of management in the light of the business cycles.

The board and the 'Black Swans': dealing with the unexpected and unknown

Typically most plans presented to the board do not take into account two key elements, both of which have profound impact on forthcoming business dynamics. First of all, by definition, most plans do not contain the occurrence and subsequent impact of unknown and unexpected events.

From time to time, the corporation is usually faced with the so-called 'Black Swans'. The concept, minted by Nassem Taleb in his book *Black Swan* (Taleb, 2010), elaborates on the unexpected and unpredictable events that can have devastating effects on both society and businesses.

Taleb defines a 'Black Swan' as an event that 'first is an outlier, as it lies outside the realm of regular expectations, because nothing in the past can conveniently point to its possibility; second, it carries an extreme impact. Third, human nature makes us concoct explanations for its occurrence after the fact, making it explainable and predictable' (Taleb, 2007).

Often, companies tend to define such 'Black Swans' as a crisis, that is, an event that through its unexpected and sudden emergence, tends to create huge problems leading to massive economic damage, and even worse, to long-term disastrous impact on both businesses and life in general.

Several senior board members pointed out during our discussions that these completely unexpected events typically did not form part of the ongoing risk analysis and management that most corporations today would be pursuing. This is where the risk analysis is then brought up to the board level, whether in the form of a proper risk assessment report carried out by external and/or internal risk managers, or through a specially dedicated Risk Committee. These exist in banks and insurance companies as a result of their regulatory situation. However, most boards outside of the financial services industry tend to conduct a regular, mostly annual, risk analysis. Regardless of whether such risk analysis and assessment has been carried out, they rarely seem to capture the truly unexpected events, or the 'Black Swans'.

It is certainly true that an identified risk, when it is resulting in an actual event, implies a situation that many times would be categorized as a crisis. In most cases where management and board regularly assess risks, such events should have been identified and their consequences predicted, so that resulting actions would be part of a contingency plan or 'Crisis Plan'.

What some companies have failed to define, however, is how the implementation of such a crisis plan should be executed. When the corporation is faced with a true 'Black Swan' event and resulting crisis, a prescribed plan for how to handle the situation may not exist. Let us look at a recent and well-known example for most readers.

During my research, I was scheduled to meet with the Chairman of BP in May of 2010. I was not surprised that the interview and meeting was being held with the Company Secretary. The meeting took place just after the Platform explosion in the Mexican Gulf.

The explosion that caused the tragic loss of life and severe damage to the local environment was by definition a 'Black Swan'. It was referred to as a crisis that would cause the board and executive management of BP to engage in a process of both trying to contain the negative effects on the environment, and also work on a solution to establish a framework to compensate the victims of the disaster.

The experience from the BP event shows the imperative of having a plan in place for how to handle even highly unlikely events. In the case of oil and gas exploration, the nature of the 'Black Swans' and their consequences is possible to define and evaluate. The most important part of such a plan to handle what could become a crisis is to define the chain of command – who does what and who communicates internally and externally.

The role of the board, its chairman and the corresponding tasks of the executive management should a 'Black Swan' occur must be defined. No organization has the luxury of time to start such planning and assignment of tasks at the time a crisis starts. Here the board must take responsibility for developing and initiating the response in the event of the 'Black Swan'.

The board and 'The Holy Cows': changing the paradigm

Management teams sometimes act as the last men on Easter Island; they drive their companies into situations where long-term prosperity is highly unlikely to ever be achieved, and even worse, where failure is a highly likely final outcome.

One senior board member of a European biomedicine company told me this frightening version of such a near death experience:

> Our CEO had proposed that we launch the new potentially revolutionary drug together with a pharmaceutical group much earlier than anybody on the R&D team or our CTO had thought was possible or viable. In fact, the results obtained from tests on animals of the potential ingredients of a virus killer drug were very positive. But together with drug companies we were involved in the early stages of trials on human beings; volunteers had been given the drug in its present shape and form but the results had yet to be analyzed very carefully. I guess the pressure from the stock market and certain shareholder groups was growing to become a situation where he simply did not have the strength to resist any longer. He had already engaged in close discussions with several pharma companies about the joint trial work, and how one of them could be awarded the rights to take the drug to market. Our business model did not include such direct commercial involvement of our own in final manufacturing, sales or distribution of a final drug. But the board had only been informed about the plan at our yearly strategy meeting six months earlier. We had given our approval to a continued process of drug development together with our selected strategic partner. The board was more concerned about our legal protection for the IP rights and possible liability exposure, not about the development of the drug itself.

The board: provider of experience and advice

Some of the companies I have been working for, in, as well as some of the companies I have founded, sometimes use a group of senior executives as a group of advisors, typically called an 'Advisory Board'. For a variety of reasons, many of these boards of senior advisors have not been able to provide the kind of advice and guidance that had been the intention from the beginning. This could be because of lack of time or commitment, or simply because of the vague definition and role of an Advisory Board. However, there are some successful exceptions.

For example, several pharmaceutical and biotech companies have been able to attract senior scientists to act as advisors in an Advisory Board. Some of these groups very successfully mix external advisors with representatives from executive management. One such example is the recently established Advisory Board of the Takeda Group of Japan.

Advisory Boards are, in fact, found in corporations across many industries. They serve as a 'sounding board' for management in terms of industry and scientific thought leadership. They are rarely taking on a proactive role in serving as a source of experience and knowledge for the corporate board or executive management.

I met a senior board member in a German industrial group. He gave me the following example of how the corporate board had created a smaller sub-group of experienced board members, a 'think tank' that had the responsibility for proactively advising management on a set of areas defined by the corporate board and executive management:

> In our group we have selected a small group of the most senior and experienced members of the Supervisory Board to form what is called the 'Senior Council'. The role of this group is to spend time in between board meetings to formulate views on a defined set of external factors that we have identified together with the management group to have the most important impact on our long term competitive position. They debate between themselves views on the state of the business cycle, on long term changes in customer preferences, on the role of emerging technologies in our served market segments and other similar long term factors having a sustainable impact on our company.

> They are especially asked to send what we call 'early warnings' should they think we are moving in a direction contradictory to their common view on long term developments. It certainly helped us to avoid the worst effects of both the technology sector downturn in the early years of the new millennium as well as what later became the worldwide financial crisis. We did not manage to avoid it completely, but thanks to their role of proactively engaging in a dialogue with executive management, I am convinced we saved a lot of severe problems that otherwise would have faced us. Several of our competitors suffered badly both in 2002–2003 and now recently in the aftermath to the financial crisis.

Interestingly, the Chairman of an Asian financial services company, presented me with a very similar concept that had been developed for his corporation:

> We ask the CEO and his management group to follow and analyze factors that impact the business of the company; both threats and opportunities. And they are constantly engaged in processes aiming at trying to predict and forecast the future and how it could impact our company. But that is not enough. Within our board we have formed a small group of senior board members. I am one of them.

He went on to say:

> All members of this group have a long experience of having faced change in what we refer to as our rules of engagement. By this we mean changes that either require a response from us, or simply that we should proactively strive to keep a continuous change process and culture of change in our organization.
> We should both act as catalysts for change; we should remind management that things do not remain in place forever, and that they must give up on their 'holy cows'! We call this small group of senior directors the 'Experience

Bank'. Just to give you an example – we recently counted that on average we had been through six recessions per board member; we hardly believed it ourselves!

The examples of the Senior Council as well as of the Experience Bank show that the more traditional concept of the Advisory Board has been further developed and refined. The experience groups have a more clearly defined mandate to intervene and reformulate strategy in the context of what could be perceived as a risk of maintaining status quo of strategy and resource allocation.

During the research, I also found an example of where such experiences were put to work in a very systematic way. One corporation has structured this process into what they call the 'Godfather Principle'. In this particular corporation, a shipping company with strong family ownership interests and historic involvement, the process has been put into system where one board member is assigned the 'Godfather' role so that all C-level executives is assigned one senior board member as his/her mentor and advisor, the 'Godfather'.

Leading through times of change and disruption: role of the board

The catalyst for change

The board should be promoting and act as a catalyst for change. Innovation should be at the core of the board's agenda. The board should constantly challenge the management team on key strategic change initiatives. This is true for innovation, new business models, new geographical markets, new product and service development as well as new growth initiatives.

Growth is a vital dimension of corporate success. Thus, a 'mantra' for growth should be fostered by the board in its interaction with management.

The value of cycles experience

The board should take on the role of monitoring the cycles; most senior board members worldwide would have firsthand experience of several business cycles. They should continue to remind management of this fact: 'what goes up, also goes down'.

This does not mean that the focus should be too short term; long-term investments must be allowed to take place even if everyone is aware that is at least one or two changes in the business environment during the lifetime of the investment. It is very hard to and should not be the task of the board to 'beat the market' in terms of timing the peaks and bottoms of an economic cycle. On the contrary, the impact of the cycles should form part of any sensible cash flow projections, forming the basis for decision-making for all investments.

However, the idea of forming a small and dedicated 'Experience Bank' or a 'Senior Council', consisting of a subset of the more experienced of the board members did prove to be highly leveraged for the corporations that had used this approach. It could also be recommended to put 'Business Cycle Plan' on the agenda for strategy retreats and as an introduction to the strategic planning process. In the end, it must be a matter of common sense for senior board members to offer their experience of having gone through cycles, to the management team.

Above all, the board must not get caught in euphoria of the false belief that there is no end to an upturn. Senior board members must not become part of a culture of ignorance and greed. This is easy to say looking back at what has occurred so many times in the past. However, it is often difficult to implement in times of immense growth and success.

The leader in crisis

Many books and articles have been written, and professional advisory services developed and offered in the area of crisis management, therefore, I will not duplicate these efforts here. I do want to point out that the board should be assigned a key role in any plan for handling a crisis when the corporation has experienced the event of a 'Black Swan'. The board has an important role to play; management is looking for experienced advice in times of a crisis.

First, it should be made clear what the tasks of the board and the executive management respectively should be. Also, communication must be managed through clearly dedicated and defined channels.

At the board level, one person should be made responsible for external communication. This role should be carefully coordinated with similar tasks having been given to executive management. No other lines of communication must exist as for the rest of the board members, this implies a time of 'radio silence'.

The challenger of the 'Holy Cows'

The 'eternal truths' that exist in most organizations, those who come from one of the extra 'Commands' previously mentioned is the saying, 'This is the way we always do things...'

These 'Holy Cows' exist in every aspect of the corporation's operations and organization. From unchallenged business models (see the Reality case on business model conversion at the department store NK), to core business processes ('this is the way we always do things'), to the role of the board ('why should we walk the extra mile?'), and similar unchallenged paradigms.

The Chairman is best suited to take the lead on the search for such perceived core pillars that could rather turn out to be holes full of quicksand. It could be best done in a close dialogue with the CEO and his team. No formal procedures are likely to discover and disclose such flaws in the corporation.

However, with common sense and using his/her previous experience, such problems should be possible to discover and correct. The key issue with the board is to make awareness that these issues are likely to exist.

The advisor

Many times, the members of the board should act ad Advisors to the management team. Senior board directors are given the task of supporting the executives with advice on strategic priorities and options, based on their own previous experiences. The mentor or 'Godfather' principle is one solution that has proven to work. The 'Experience Bank' is another way of structuring the transfer of knowhow and experience from the board to the executive management level. Finally, the principles behind the more traditional Advisory Board could also be applied to the corporate board.

However, it requires a dedicated small group of board members in order to work. Such strong leadership is also appreciated outside the company. In fact, it has been proven to have a significant impact on the value creation for the company. This is shown in a recent study, *Leadership Premium*, published in 2012 by Deloitte. According to Deloitte, market perceptions of leaders can raise company valuations by as much as 16 per cent.

Whereas market analysts have in the past focused largely on financial risk and reward, recent calamities have led to an increased focus on the risk of leadership failure and the importance of leadership quality. *The Leadership Premium* report details the core capabilities analysts use to measure the quality of leadership. It also puts a hard metric on the 'intangible asset' of leadership, and shows that, in some sectors, good leaders can account for more than one-fifth of equity value.

The report, based on a survey of leading market analysts in the UK, the US, China, India, Japan, and Brazil reveals that the quality of senior leadership, both core capabilities as well as personal qualities such as honesty and integrity, have a measurable impact on analysts' assessments of a company's current performance and its potential for future success and sustainability. The board has a key role to play in assuming leadership to take the corporation through good and bad times, to encourage and lead through change.

The results in the Deloitte report (Deloitte Touche Tohmatsu Limited (DTTL), *The Leadership Premium* [March 2012]) show that the gap between the value of a company with good leadership and that of a company with weaker leadership could be more than 35 per cent. The report indicates that there are three core components that are key when assessing an organization's leadership strength: strategic clarity, and successful execution, and a culture of innovation.

In addition, according to the Deloitte research, there are two attributes that support these components, effective corporate governance and effective leadership characteristics. These core capabilities, as well as personal qualities such as honesty and integrity, have a measurable impact on analysts' assessments of a company's current performance and its potential for future success and

Reality case

Guiding through cycles

The board of this large European food group formed a small group that is not a formal sub-committee of the board, nor does it form an official part of the board. It takes few minutes to meet and the number of board members in the group is limited to four.

The members are the most senior directors of the supervisory board. Those of the board members who have the longest and most extensive experience of how changes in the general economy and long terms trends in society could affect business. They are senior executives with experience not only from the food industry, but from business in general.

One of the members had described this group for me as the 'Experience Bank'. He was very firm in explaining that the task for this group was not to formulate or discuss strategy or review existing strategic initiatives. It was certainly not a sub-committee of the board with a specific role to perform that otherwise could have been handled by the board. Instead, its primary task was to evaluate the impact of the ongoing crisis in the Eurozone on the long term-growth strategy of the group.

One of the group members was the chairman of the group, but he did not chair the meeting that was taking place this afternoon and evening in Paris. The group had decided to meet at a small resort hotel outside of the city. Both phone calls and e-mail exchanges were strongly discouraged. Each one of the members was asked to give his/her view on the crisis and where it would lead to. The group agreed on one issue already after the first round of introductions; the exiting crisis would prolong the recession that had come so soon after the previous one. In fact, all four members had to admit that none of them had ever experienced anything like this crisis in their previous careers.

The purpose of the discussions and thus the justification for the meeting was to provide the management team with some guidelines ahead of the upcoming strategic planning process that the company performed every year. More importantly, it gave the entire board a basis for evaluating some of the forthcoming proposals for strategic initiatives that the management team was about to prepare.

The group was aware of that the management team had their own group of experts and staff managers who had been working on similar tasks. The major difference from this ongoing environmental analysis and the corporate planning process was that the output from the senior board member group would only serve to guide the board in the decision-making process on strategic growth options to be proposed by management. After several hours of intense discussions, the group sat down to formulate a set of guidelines that they would present at the next board meeting.

The group summarized their views in a set of headings:

- Impact of the crisis on general purchasing power of customers
- Differences between geographical markets within Europe
- Impact on long-term preferences for food consumption
- A view on the possible duration and outcome of the crisis

Typically, the board would allocate two hours at the next board meeting for discussion of the impact of the conclusions from the 'Experience Bank' on strategy for the corporation going forward. To this part of the board meeting, the chairman and CEO would invite selected members of the entire top management team.

Lessons to be learned

Reality case: 'Guiding through Cycles'

- A key role of the board is to provide executive management with experiences and common sense.
- Most board members should have been part of several business cycles. They should know the 'what goes up eventually goes down' – and remind management of this and guide the CEO and his/her team through periods of change and disruption.
- The board should challenge the 'Holy Cows' that might prevail in the organization.

CHAPTER 8

Value creation through innovation: the role of the board

During one of my interviews with a chairmen of a large corporation regarding to what extent his board was actively pursuing innovation in the corporation, he answered, 'Yes, we regularly check the R&D spending and we have a yearly board session where we discuss and approve next year's R&D budget.'

> Another chairman gave a similar view on the board and its role in pursuing innovations: Innovation at Board level [is] not our responsibility. Instead we approve budgets and appoint the CTO based on proposals from the CEO. We know too little about technology and research at the Board…. This [innovation] is not my cup of tea, nor is it for the Board to engage in.

This attitude and similar opinions based on the belief that innovation comes from research in the traditional sense of product and technology development is deeply rooted in the minds of many corporate executives, and amongst board members of the same companies. However, one chairman of a large Asian industrial conglomerate told this interesting approach, 'We [the directors] constantly ask for new solutions and ways to do business. We challenge the CEO and his team with questions about the 'Holy Cows' that they promote in the traditional approach to our business. Instead, we want new disruptive ways to engage with competition and to serve our customers, both existing and new.'

There are many reasons why the first two comments are not only wrong but also could be deemed as being signs of a very dangerous approach to innovation in corporations. Some of the underlying assumptions behind such arguments are biased because of the assumption that innovation is only derived from systematic and structured research and development (R&D) efforts through established and dedicated R&D resources. A similarly biased belief is that innovation is only derived from technology and product development efforts, whereas innovation can also be linked to developing new customer solutions, new innovative design of core processes, new and disruptive business models and so on. In this case, the overall view of the board is that there is not a need to play an active role in pursuing innovations throughout the organization.

Instead, reflect on the comment made by the chairman of the Asian group. It shows a very different approach to innovation in general and that of the role of a board in innovation in particular. Innovation is not merely linked to technology and product but is just as much related to finding new solutions for core process design, new innovative customer solutions and new business models. Pursuing innovation and challenging existing solutions (the 'Holy Cows') is a key task of a corporate board, and not only for the CEO and his team, albeit execution must be done at management level; the board sets the framework for the innovation efforts, and creates an innovation driven culture in the organization.

In 1985, Peter Drucker made this important comment on innovation: '... innovation therefore consists in the purposeful and organized search for change, and in the systematic analysis of the opportunities such changes might offer for economic or social innovation'.

Constantinos Markides (LBS, 2008) as well as Kim and Mauborgne (INSEAD, 2005), have developed the concept of innovation further along these lines. Markides argues that business model innovation should be seen as different from technological innovation and thus exploited in a different way, '... innovation is not one thing. It comes in different types – product, technological, business model, and so on – all of which are capable of creating new market space'.

This more business-oriented view on innovation, as being the provider of new solutions, was shared by some of the chairmen interviewed. However, most senior executives tended to regard innovation as the more traditional research-based process.

One of the most innovation-oriented boards encountered was from a European microelectronics multinational. Its chairman noted:

> We have an agenda item for innovation that is included for every board meeting during the year. In addition, once a year, during the annual Board Strategy Retreat, we always spend one entire session on innovation and new innovative solutions, both technical and business driven. This has resulted in a strong focus on innovation and challenging the paradigms amongst the management team that is always present during the retreat session. It is a true value lever.

A comprehensive view on innovation from a board perspective

How can innovation be defined so as to become a key element of the board's modus operandi? As many of the academics who have done research in the area of innovation have concluded, there is no single answer to this question. However, to help define a relevant and more extensive definition of what we mean by innovation in this context, let us draw upon findings of some of the scholars in the past, as well as use input

Value creation through innovation

based on the experience-sharing and fact-finding interview sessions with the chairmen and CEO's from this research.

A definition of innovation for the purpose of engaging the board in the pursuit and promotion of innovation can be outlined as:

- Pursuing new solutions to meet changing customer needs; this requires that both the business as well as product development efforts are being closely linked to the customer interface of the organization.
- Developing new and (sometimes) disruptive business models that offer customers new benefits and differentiates the offering from competition.
- Looking for new inventions, often technical in nature, that are the result of systematic research for new ideas and breakthroughs.
- Encouraging on-going research and experimentation to focus on new applications and processes.
- Exploiting the unexpected and disruptive discoveries, the 'Black Swans' of innovation, albeit bearing in mind that such major innovations are not common and by definition hard to make embedded into the ongoing traditional R&D efforts.

Only by realizing that innovation efforts can be pursued in different ways can the board engage in successful innovation efforts. As the Chairman of a UK conglomerate put it during our discussion:

> It is clearly not up to the Board to execute and deliver on new innovations; but we could formulate the 'Leitmotif' and set the goals and provide the role models; leading the operating organization to aspire to create extraordinary results; show that nothing is impossible and that we accept failures that happened because the goal was to achieve new innovations. We at Board level could set the goals and provide the resources; then it is up to management and the organization to deliver.

The board and the innovation-oriented corporation

By adopting a wider view on innovation and how and from where innovation emerges, the board can engage in the enhancement and enrichment of the innovation process itself. The overall role of the board in promoting and leveraging innovation to generate sustainable and business-driven results is to engage in the creation of an innovation-oriented culture throughout the organization.

Innovation must be seen as a way to meet customer needs by offering new and value- based solutions. As we have seen, most successful innovations are driven by such customer-oriented offerings. Good examples are the recent success of Apple and its iPhone, iPod and iPad series combined with the already established Mac models; the new successful business models offered by several low cost airlines such as Easyjet, Ryanair, Norwegian, Southwest and JetBlue. There are many other similar examples of successful new innovations, all representing different forms of new thinking and offerings.

Although actual development efforts will have to remain the responsibility of the CEO and his/her C-line executives, the board can play a key role in enabling the emergence and growth of such an innovation-oriented organization. By pressing chairmen and CEOs to describe how they have been involved in various forms of innovation initiatives, the following typical roles were identified as:

- Acting as a source of inspiration for management, by communicating the value of innovation, how the board puts innovation at the forefront of business development, and using success stories and role models as examples both within and outside the corporation.
- Structuring a process whereby the traditional views and models (the 'Holy Cows') are being challenged and new solutions are being promoted and put in focus for the entire organization.

- Rewarding innovations and innovative behaviour, thus encouraging the organization to dare to 'think-out-of-the-box' and emphasize that failures when pursuing new ideas and solutions are acceptable and even should be encouraged as long as they are aimed at creating new and customer-oriented initiatives.
- Facilitating innovations and the emergence and development of new solutions; both by creating organizational solutions to such innovation efforts (see below), such as incubators and other physically distinct organizational units.
- Providing the resources, both financial and human, to engage in the innovation efforts; however, not only by the simplistic approval of a yearly R&D budget as mentioned by the chairman previously quoted, but by ear-marking and leveraging key organizational resources and encouraging the CEO and his/her C-level team, (not just the CTO and Chief Engineer) to invest these into innovation-focused initiatives.

A Chairman in a Swedish telecom company put it this way to me:

> It is all about customer focus; realizing that customers, both existing and new, request new solutions. By always asking the question 'are we doing the right things for our customers?', you create a culture of understanding true needs and key issues facing them, and hence these insights can subsequently turn into new innovative solutions to resolve them.

Role of the board in innovation-based value creation

The key imperative for the board in promoting and implementing an innovation-based organization and culture is to set the goals and create role models through pursuing successful innovation initiatives. The board should encourage the ongoing search for change to develop solutions to customer needs and strategic issues. This effort must be implemented through the organization and management, only in exceptional cases should the board members be directly involved in the actual innovation efforts and initiatives.

There are some concrete initiatives and themes that the board can and should pursue to promote and enhance innovation. A good starting point is to put innovation on the board agenda as suggested by one of the chairmen previously. Elaborating on innovation-related themes as part of the overall strategy process where the board is engaged is another such imperative. All of these actions must be carefully coordinated with executive management and the CEO must buy into the proposed actions and efforts. Without such acceptance of the initiatives and their rationale for value creation, there are huge risks of creating typical 'not invented here' reactions.

This is a key challenge for the chairman to implement together with the CEO and his team prior to proposing such action items to the board for evaluation and decision. During the interviews with the chairmen in the research study, we encountered a set of initiatives where the board could play a key role in launching and supporting innovation-based value creation initiatives.

- If deemed relevant, the board could decide on the creation of specific organizational entities for dedicated innovation. What Markides calls 'The Separation Strategy', he refers to the well-known examples of the separation of the Nespresso business unit from the rest of the Nestlé core organization into a separate entity, which was also physically moved to another location apart from the rest of the Nestlé group.
- We know how successful the Nespresso initiative proved to be. This was a key board decision based on recommendations from executive management. There are many other examples of both successful dual business units pursuing separate business models. There are quite a few examples of failures resulting from such separation initiatives as well. Some are well known, such as the IBM failed Ambra

Value creation through innovation

initiative (as discussed in the following section), British Airways and GO, KLM and Buzz, and several other unsuccessful separation initiatives. The board must evaluate a proposal to launch a separate business model in a separate organizational unit based on its own merits, balancing the pros and cons against each other. While this is possible, it does require a delicate balance so as not to alienate the existing core organization and thus risk a severe disruption of on-going business activities.

- Another such organizational initiative used to bolster innovation, is the creation of separate organizational units dedicated for innovation in adjacent or even unrelated areas, both technology-based as well as customer solutions-based. Some large industrial groups have been pursuing such incubator units as well as dedicated in-house laboratories and even production lines to test out and prove new and disruptive innovations that fall outside of the existing core business. Some of these initiatives have been successful in developing new and emerging solutions and technologies. Whereas others have been forced to close down because of lack of success and after having consumed massive resources or even caused a clear distraction from the core business development. An example of such a failed initiative is the attempt by IBM to develop a low-cost PC in the mid-1990s, the so-called Ambra project. Again, this is an area where the board could take a proactive role, propose such solutions to executive management and work in tandem with them to implement such initiatives if deemed relevant.

Similarly, some large industrial groups have established corporate venture capital arms, with the aim of financing and growing new innovations that over time can be integrated with the core business areas. Intel Capital is a successful example of such a corporate VC initiative. Nokia Ventures has been a similar vehicle for Nokia to invest in early-stage wireless technology start-ups with the intent to grow these to scale and then integrate them into the core business organization. Others have experienced less positive results and have either been sold off or been forced to close down. One such example was the venture arm of Swedish telecom operator Telia (now TeliaSonera) in its Venture Capital (VC) arm Telia Business Innovation.

- When presented with such schemes, the board must carefully evaluate to the extent such venture investments can be integrated with the core. There is no clear role model for how a successful corporate venture investment activity should be structured and implemented. The board needs to act with prudence and care.
- There are some examples where large corporations have implemented a systematic approach to promote innovation through encouraging and supporting intrapreneurship (that is, behaving like an entrepreneur, except within a larger organization). Such initiatives should be sanctioned and encouraged by the board to mark the strategic significance of the initiative. The effectiveness of intrapreneurship initiatives are yet to be fully evaluated, but they should evolve from a strong innovation-oriented culture, as previously discussed.
- The board should promote and present successful role models for innovation throughout the organization. This is one of the discussion points for the board where innovation was one of the standing agenda points for their board meetings. Either the chairman or another board member with a specific task of engaging in and following up on innovation initiatives, could select and present such role models based on successful innovations that have been successfully developed and implemented in the corporation. This is typically the task of the CEO and his/her team, but by giving the board an active role, the symbolic effect of its engagement and commitment to innovation is reinforced. It becomes similar to what Sandra Vandermerwe of Tanaka/Imperial College, describes in her research as the 'Points of Light'. Starting at board level, a strong message and insight is being sent through the actions and behaviour of top management. Vandermerwe refers to customer-oriented behaviour and actions, although her theory applies to innovation-oriented

Value creation through innovation

behaviour as well, using the comprehensive extended definition of innovation that was previously presented.
- Finally, the board has a defined responsibility to integrate externally generated innovations into the corporation, primarily through negotiating strategic partnerships around R&D and innovation-oriented initiatives around intellectual property, through cross-licensing arrangements, as well as through dedicated M&A efforts to acquire and subsequently integrate adjacent and synergistic solutions and technologies to add to its own core competencies.

Implications for value creating boards

In summary, the research has shown that the board could and should play a proactive role in inspiring, supporting and providing resources for new innovations. Such innovations could be of different nature, and by adapting such an extended definition of innovation, particularly regarding offering new innovative solutions to customer needs and requirements, the board could engage in initiatives as previously described, and thus create real and sustainable value for the corporation.

The key is for the board to work together with executive management to create and sustain an innovation-oriented culture throughout the entire organization. Also, for them to act accordingly by creating and promoting successful innovation in the form of role models for the corporation it serves.

Reality case

Board and innovation – the conversion at NK, a Swedish department store

This Reality case takes place in the board room of NK, Sweden's leading department store. The board is gathering for a key meeting in the early months of 1990. NK CEO Raoul Hasselgren is putting together his new strategy for his upcoming presentation to his board. He is going to propose a fundamental change of the existing traditional business model for NK. He has prepared the presentation very carefully as he knows that his proposal will be subject to an intense strategy discussion between the various board members. However, he has prewired his chairman, Bernt Magnusson, CEO of Nordstjernan, the largest owner of NK, and at least the initial reaction to his plan has been received in a positive way. But who knows how the entire board will respond.

In brief, the background of NK can be summarized as: NK was the first department store in Sweden, and opened its first store in 1902. Its founder and owner, Josef Sachs, moved into its present location in central Stockholm in 1915. Similar to many other department stores based on the traditional business concept of selling a wide range of products in one single store location, often with the idea of shopping 'all under one roof'. Originating from the nineteenth century, early stores were Au Bon Marché and Galeries Lafayette in Paris, Selfridges in London, and later on Harrods, Bloomingdale's, Macy's, Kaufhof and many others worldwide.

During the 1980s, NK was facing an increasingly difficult retail market and was underperforming against other retail stores and chains such as H&M and IKEA. This led the board of NK to evaluate new strategic options for sustainable and long-term profitable growth. One option, to merge NK with other leading Scandinavian department stores, had been analysed and subsequently rejected.

The other strategic option had been defined by Raoul Hasselgren with a small group of consultants who together with him had studied some recent experiences from conversion of the traditional department store business model into a new business concept and model. For almost ten years, NK had successfully rented store space to a small group of brand retailers who offered smaller ranges of their own brands in a dedicated 'shop in shop' or 'concessions' at NK. The return from this rental operation exceeded that of NK's own traditional department store activities.

Value creation through innovation

Raoul Hasselgren had put together the strategy and financial plan into a business plan into what was called 'The Entrepreneur Department Store'. The new business model was based on a version of a franchising concept with a combination of retailers and tenants, where NK managed the store and did not use its own staff or inventory, but where the strong brand name NK offered a significant strength to the overall proposition.

The new business model was to be rolled out in the flagship store in Stockholm and in the second largest store in Gothenburg, Sweden's second largest city. Other NK stores were closed down.

The selection of brands and tenants was based on a mix of fashion wear and various products that could normally be found in a department store, that is, apparel, suits, accessories, kitchenware, furniture, interiors, perfume, cosmetics and so on. However, this time these were to be offered through specialized retailers. The goal was to offer the customer an experience like an event attraction. Thus, the store also housed restaurants, coffee shops, bars and so on.

All marketing and advertising had to follow a common framework and graphic design, called 'The Profile Book'. This new model had not been tested in Sweden before and very few examples of the fully developed concept existed.

Prior to the board meeting, Raoul Hasselgren had briefed the board members individually, and had gotten an informal 'go ahead' from the chairman. Still, he was not sure of the final outcome of the meeting's decision. The board meeting was successful. The board approved of the new business model and gave its 'green light' to launch the 'Entrepreneur Department Store' or the new NK.

The initial public opinion and media reactions were highly sceptical. But, reality proved Hasselgren to have been right. Revenue growth for the first five years after the conversion was 50 per cent. The new business concept had become a clear success.

Lessons to be learned

Reality case: 'Conversion at NK – A Swedish Department Store'

- The board should constantly monitor the business model of the corporation.
- If deemed to lead to stagnation and loss of competitive position, the board must act to push management for innovation and rethinking of business model.
- Such fundamental change of strategy and business model must be based on solid analysis and include a joint commitment of board and management.

Chapter 9
Boosting peak performance

The law of performance

All organizations are supposed to perform and provide results to their various stakeholders, as indeed are all human beings to themselves. In the corporate world, and in the prevailing world of market dynamics, the key performance indicators tend to be defined as returns on various resources, or assets, deployed to create these same returns. Returns are impacted by the actions of people, employees and executives of the corporation. The higher the returns are, the better the performance.

This 'Law of Performance', whether measured in return on assets or investment, or in relative terms such as market share and degree of sustainability, are all subject to the actions and decisions taken by the people in the organization or corporation.

In most corporations, both private and public, certain established performance levels seem to have been accepted as either being excellent, good, poor or bad. When studying company presentations and reading interviews with CEOs, certain norms seem to exist and are being used without very much reflection and clear adjustments to what represents full potential for the specific business at stake. For example, a statement like this is common practice among many corporate communication channels today: 'We aim at achieving a return on capital employed of 15%.'

It sounds good, but the fact is that there are far too many corporations that state more or less the same goal. The same thing applies to growth targets such as 'We should grow at 10% per year over a business cycle', and other similar statements, or profitability targets such as 'Our target is to achieve an EBITDA margin of 12%', as well as other such indicators of performance drivers.

In fact, based on having discussed performance-related issues with many of the chairmen in this study, there is a clear trend that performance target setting and evaluation is being handled in a spirit of 'muddling through'. An attitude such as 'this is good enough', or, what some chairmen called 'satisfactory underperformance', and several established practices such as 'benchmarking' all add to the creation of a culture where the notion of superior performance to reach the full potential, has been forgotten or never allowed to exist in the first place.

As one Chairman of a highly successful global food group told me: 'Benchmarking is for losers; winners focus on creating a gap [a performance gap to competition]'. This specific Chairman has a highly successful record of consistently outperforming competition. He claims it is thanks to a very clearly articulated focus on performance improvement and the search for excellence in all aspects of the value chain of the corporation. This Chairman then added, 'Mediocre performance can never be tolerated; but at the same time, clearly mistakes must be allowed. We must never confuse poor performance records with results, even negative, coming from taking on entrepreneurial risk and the pursuit of innovation.'

Therefore, setting the performance targets and managing the follow up through a systematic performance evaluation process are the key dimensions of management and leadership. Here the board must also play a leading role.

One can draw a parallel from the private equity world, where active ownership and an extreme focus on performance in order to create value in the portfolios of the private equity investment firms, are the guiding principles for governance and management. The star performers of the private equity industry are those firms that set the highest standards for maximizing the operating value of the underlying businesses among their portfolio companies. Some chairmen, board members and senior executives of successful corporations are applying the same performance oriented approach to governance and leadership; they preach and obey the 'Law of Performance'. In this case, the board could and should play a leading role in establishing and pursuing such a performance-based culture and core business practices.

Let us now turn to how the board can perform such performance-boosting tasks in a corporation, regardless of the nature of ownership. Here we focus on situations where the board is doing just the opposite to boost performance of the business. For example, how the board contributes to damage or even destroys a performance-based culture in a high-performing organization, and thus never allows it to reach even a fraction of its full potential. There were some examples of such value depreciating boards in the sample of companies taking part in the research. In these companies, the boards had a very negative impact on the performance of the corporation, because of the incompetence or lack of insight and leadership.

How the board can damage or 'kill' a performance-based culture

Far too many boards tend to damage the performance of a company and even destroy the value that otherwise could have been created by the corporation. One CEO in an advanced telecom technology group complained to me:

> My board does not allow me to think big. I present so many bold strategies and key strategic initiatives, for example to acquire competitors or complementary product manufacturers, or to enter new geographical markets. But they do not allow me to undertake such growth moves. They claim

that it would have a negative impact on the short term performance of our stock price. This is the only thing that matters for my board; keep the stock price rising every month, every quarter. I try to convince them that my proposed actions would create huge value for shareholders in the long term. But so far, they have not changed their opinion. It is such a shame. I almost hope that a private equity fund could buy us out from the stock exchange.

Lack of long-term strategic vision and 'trivial pursuit' of drivers of short-term stock price increases are two key errors that are very common among public company boards. Linked to this lack of long-term focus, is the failure to define the organization: what could it really achieve? What are the relevant targets for long-term performance? Part of such negligence to communicate long-term goals is linked to the short-term focus, driven by capital market concerns, which is the impact on short-term stock price movements. The conclusion, supported by the view of many top executives, is that the long-term goals and targets are not linked to what is really achievable. As another CEO for a public company put it:

> As long as we perform well enough, they [the board] leave us alone and do not seem to be concerned or even interested. We ask for more bold targets but never get these by our board. The chairman is content as long as we are doing better than the average performer on the main board [the London Stock Exchange]. Our potential is bigger than the targets reflect.

This attitude of 'laissez-faire' is typical for many boards; a culture of tolerance for 'satisfactory underperformance' or 'good enough' performance seems to prevail in many corporations. I am convinced that this avoidance of definition and asking what is the true performance potential, costs shareholders vast amounts of lost value and opportunity.

A third reason for why boards fail to promote performance is the failure to design and implement a reward system linked to (a correctly defined) performance target. This issue is not new and has been debated for a long time among corporate executives, among board members and by academic thought leaders. Everybody seems to agree that a correctly designed reward system would encourage management to improve performance to reach those targets that would trigger the rewards.

One chairman of a large food nutrition group described it this way:

> We [the board] set out to define performance targets that would align management at all levels with the overall strategic goals of our corporation. It worked fantastically; we were able to increase performance both for operations, and our bottom line. An important achievement was the dramatically improved rate of new innovations that was the result of the new design.

This particular company had developed a reward system that offered incentives to managers both for the short- and the long-term. A long-term incentive system is a key element in the performance-based organization. But only for a system that reflects true value creation. We only have to go back to the 2008 financial crisis to understand how wrongly designed incentive systems also foster dangerous behaviour, and in the case of some players in the financial system, spilled over into greediness and a focus on enrichment of the individual, not the corporation he/she served.

Fourth, the lack of relevant competences and skills of the board and/or the chairman seem to be a key factor for negative performance. One chairman stated:

> I am the only director on this board who has any experience from the industry we are in. It is a very lonely and sometimes hopeless task to inform the other members about what the business is all about. Even if sometimes their questions raise issues that we tend to ignore. But I would prefer a situation where most board members had

at least a hint about what the industry landscape is all about. A lot of time at board meetings is used for pure information and knowledge sharing.

Sometimes this leads to the 'PowerPoint Waterfalls' where the management team shows vast amount of slides just describing the basics of their business area for the board. One CEO explained during an interview about his interaction with the board:

> They [the board] do not understand the business. They have no clue what we should be doing and if we fail or succeed. I do not think anybody on the board has a serious business background, and the few directors who do, seem to lack industry knowledge and insight in any case. It is simply very frustrating but I cannot really do anything about it, can I?

The interviews clearly showed the great difference between boards where the directors had a high degree of competence and insight and those where no such skills existed. A recent example of lack of industry insight worth considering is the composition of the Board of Lehman Brothers at the time leading up to the bank's collapse and subsequent bankruptcy. With the exception of its Chairman and CEO, Dick Fuld and the CFO of the bank who reported to the board, very few, if any, of the board members of Lehman Brothers had a significant background in banking and particularly not in investment banking,. And we all now know what happened to Lehman Brothers.

Creating value through a systematic approach to boosting performance

A key role for the board is to exercise leadership and to do everything it can to boost the performance of the corporation. Based on the extensive interviews with the group of distinguished chairmen and senior executives during the research, the following conclusions and subsequent recommendations for how a board can create value for the corporation through boosting performance and hence creating a performance-based culture in the organization.

The insightful board

One chairman told during a five hour long interview in the group's head office:

> I know I should learn more about the company and especially about what drives operating performance. But I must figure out ways how I should receive the right kind of information, where and when. I could get as much as I want and need, but it is too much. Sometimes I wish I had an editor who could condense and prepare the relevant information for me ahead of board meetings. But even then it would not be enough. The CEO and his team will always have a clear advantage of possessing superior information; I must rely on them and trust their judgement. But still I sometimes feel like I should know more and gain more insider knowledge about the business and its performance.

Therefore, getting the right information and getting it in a structured and systematic format and process, is a prerequisite for a board to exercise leadership and add value to the corporation. Then, the board must use this knowledge in a way so that it helps boost performance of the management team. They do this by setting examples and knowing lots about the business and its value drivers. One chairman told the following interesting story:

> Our CEO came to the board and reported that he had beaten his peers in industry by achieving an EBITDA margin of 15%, 'We are best in our industry', he told the board. But we told him to go back and do better. He agreed with some degree of reluctance. And then he came

back a couple of months later and claimed that he now was at 18% on an on-going basis. Still, we at the board were not satisfied with the result. 'Go back and do your homework again' we told him. He came back again after six months and announced with lots of pride that he/they had now reached an EBITDA of more than 20%. The board decided to say OK to this, but we had to tell him that we had expected him to be at 25% instead. He was confused and asked how we could tell him so. I replied on behalf of the entire board that we had three reasons for our more aggressive targets. 'First', we told him, 'your CSG costs are too high and could be lowered by at least 10%; second, your distribution system is too complex and you should be able to decrease working capital build-up by at least 5%. And third, the company should consider a more dynamic approach to pricing decisions to better capture fluctuations in supply and demand'. Our CEO first seemed confused, then nodded and accepted our challenge. He realized that we both understood his business model and strategy, and hence that we seriously could add value to his leadership and hence the performance of the business he managed. Since this point in time, we have tended to outperform competition on a consistent basis.

This is a fundamental statement; obviously the board in this case created real value through its interactive engagement with the CEO and his team. It is an example of a successful approach to value-based board leadership.

Only when the board is in possession of such information and knowledge, can it pursue an active role in goal and target formulation, definition of full potential, and evaluate the true performance of management and the business.

This calls for a set of key imperatives:

1. A well-*functioning information gathering and delivery process*. The board must receive the relevant information in a systematic and intelligent fashion; no 'data dumps' or, even worse, being presented with huge amount of new

information at board meetings by various business managers, the so called 'PowerPoint Waterfalls' as expressed by one chairman in an interview.
2. A composition of the board so that at least a core group of board members possess the *relevant skills and necessary insight* concerning the business of the corporation. The days are over when board memberships were handed out as an award for past services; a modern board member must not only understand his/her duties from a governance perspective, but also have the skills and knowledge required to guide and support the management team running the company.

The pursuit of true potential

The chairman of a large Asian industrial group told me:

> We spend a lot of time defining the true potential of our business lines; we ask the management team 'What could you really achieve with the business you are leading?' We ask them to come back and tell us what they could achieve both by boosting operating performance and effectiveness, and how to leverage their strategic position through pursuing bold growth strategies. It sends a clear message to the management team that they are free to 'think big'. This has really worked very well for us, and we have developed a process for how to assess true potential and also for how to draw the roadmap leading to obtaining it. We at the board strongly believe in this process. It also requires us at the board to do our homework, to really understand what is do-able and what should be required from the team.
> It works two ways, as an interaction between the board and the management team, and everybody is happy with this approach. You could argue that it has replaced our traditional strategic planning process. For good I hope.

But the successful companies pursuing the true potential of their business are not only concerned with defining what the true potential is or should be. They also spend lots of time to develop the plan, or 'Roadmap' as the chairman previously stated, for how to achieve the true potential. At first glance, this may seem no different from the more traditional strategic planning processes used by many companies. But the difference is that the board by asking for the 'true potential' implicitly tells the management team that just 'good' is not good enough. That 'good could always be done better'. By asking for the true or full potential, the goals are set even higher than 'better'.

A the chairman of this North European maritime group told me:

> We want to be 'Simply the Best'. This desire we have in our company, colours the entire organization. We want to hire the best talent; we want to offer them the best rewards. But we only do it for 'best in class' performance. Our managers know this, and they are aligned with this overall paradigm. It works.

Therefore, definition of true potential is what the corporation should be able to accomplish, the 'best in class' performance targets. This requires that the board sets the rules of the exercise, and tells the management team that it must 'think big' or 'out-of-the-box'.

Many times this is a hard task. The 'reality check' that must be in place can easily hamper a bold strategic approach with too ambitious targets and goals. But the exercise in itself has a considerable value to enhance the quality of strategic thinking of the management team. A key outcome is the new performance-based culture that the process brings about.

Drawing the performance roadmap

Having established the goals and targets for true potential, the board should go on to ask the management team how they intend to get there, to define the 'roadmap' that the chairman stated in the previous quote. The corporations using the roadmap technique tend to focus on two dimensions of performance enhancement:

1. Strategic initiatives such as mergers and acquisitions, penetration of new geographical markets, disruptive innovations, development of new strategic partnerships and joint ventures, and even rethinking of traditional business models.
2. Actions to improve the operating effectiveness of the corporation.

By keeping a high level of ambition for the exercise and stretching the imagination of what could be done, the management team is seen to emphasize superior performance. They are starting to create the Gap. The role of the board is to ask for this deliverable, and to set the framework and expectations for the process. It should determine the 'rules of engagement'.

What the board could do for you

One chairman said during an interview in her head office:

> We have been so used to the board setting the goals and requesting the CEO to deliver the results. That is of course still the case, but in our company we have started a dialogue with the management team, where we try to create a two-way 'give-and-take' atmosphere. We ask the CEO to come back to us with a statement of 'We ask what you can do for your company and its board'; now we [the board], ask 'what can the board do for you?' This has inspired a very fruitful dialogue about resource commitments and the active role of the board in supporting the CEO and his team.

This is the board in a very successful company that is asking the CEO and his team to come back and ask what the board could do for them. Typically, the process is the opposite; the board expects the management team to deliver and the board to monitor and evaluate the deliverables.

In some of the corporations researched, the board encouraged the management team to ask the board members what the board could contribute to the fulfilment of the full potential, to implement the 'roadmap'. The chairman of a industrial group stated:

> It reminds me a little bit of the 'chicken-and-egg' situation; the goals we set are only realistic if there is a realistic plan available to reach them; and the plan is only possible to implement, if the relevant resources are made available to the business. Thus, instead of either a 'top-down' or a 'bottom-up' process, we try to pursue a parallel and iterative approach, where the management team will ask the board for resources as a key input to the planning process. Not just the overall performance goals. It works but requires a little bit more time and close interaction between me and the CEO.

Only if the relevant resources are offered to the management for its disposal, could the team validate how realistic and relevant the roadmap is.

Aligning the rewards

This is the statement of one board member of an electronics group.

> Normally, it is easy to set goals and monitor performance. But unless we recognize the achievements of management and their organization, and reward them accordingly, we will never get to where we should be. We have worked very, very hard to design and agree on a system for rewarding the performance levels we want to see in our company. Our rule of thumb has been simplicity and

a visible link between effort and results, all integrated in a transparent system that is deemed to be fair by everybody. It is based on individual as well as team based performance. It is a must for us to stimulate top performance and achievements.

He continued:

> Not only do we want to have a fair and attractive reward system in place, but we also note that increasingly this is becoming a request from the younger generations of top talent that we try to attract to our organization. Yes, we compete for talent, and the design and functioning of our reward system has become a key competitive tool for winning these contests for the best talent available. We cannot survive long term without these stars.

The management literature is full of thought leadership on this topic, so I do not dwell on the subject in this book. But it is a theme that engages the executives and board members interviewed, who spent many long hours discussing the issues related to performance measurement and follow up, and the reward systems needed to back them up.

It is a well-documented fact that successful corporations are able to retain their top talent and increase effectiveness and results coming from such a motivated organization. A board must play a key role in the design and implementation of such an aligned reward system, and never take loyalty from the top managers for granted. Loyalty is a core asset of any company, and it must be managed and given the careful attention it requires and deserves.

Boosting the culture of peak performance

Several chairmen identified this task as the key imperative for all boards; to engage with the management team in a 'win-win' process that both inspires, boosts, and retains a management culture where performance is at the very core of the values and driving forces. This is a process where the board sets out to boost a winning performance oriented culture, the one that focuses on 'creating the Gap'.

This is easy to say but not so easy to achieve. So what did the research tell about the top performers in this context? Are there ways through which a board can act in a planned and systematic way to boost top performance? Can a true performance-based culture be developed and maintained over time? The conclusion from the research is 'Yes it can'.

Although every board and almost every chairman pointed at their own 'secrets' for how to achieve this, at least among those where performance was a priority, there seems to be some common themes that can be found at the high performing corporations met with in this research. The successful performance 'boosters' always focus on 'true potential' and push the CEO and his/her team towards achieving this level of performance.

- The boards of these companies did not tolerate excuses such as 'it happened to us'; the focus is on proactive behaviour.
- The development and agreement of the 'roadmap' to reach peak performance is a key element in the boosting of top performing companies; here the board must play a leading role and be very well prepared.
- The board sets high and frequently tough targets for management, but they can justify these based on its understanding of their relevance, and also support the CEO and his/her team to achieve them, based on their own knowledge and insight.
- By having an excellent understanding of the business and its key value drivers, and by sharing these insights with management, a *mutual respect and trust* is established. This is a key prerequisite for building the performance culture.
- This superior understanding of and insight into the value drivers of the business is a prerequisite but does not come

easy. There are two key initiatives required to create the 'insightful board':
- By designing a relevant and user adapted information system allowing for real-time interaction between board and management if required.
- By carefully deciding on the optimal composition and profile of the board members themselves, and by letting them act as 'One Team'.

- Finally, the spirit of the pursuit of 'peak performance' must colour the actions and *modus operandi* of the board. This is captured by the final remarks of one of the chairmen who explained, 'I have an excellent CEO and he is working with a super smart team. They are always reaching the highest possible standards. But nevertheless, I and my board want to see even better results. We are convinced that "Good can always be done better"'.

Reality case

Performance focus

The constant pursuit of superior performance

We are observers at the meeting of the Board of a US retail store chain. The meeting is held in the board room at the head office of the group. The company has recently been bought by one of the largest private equity firms in the country. The new owners have put in place a smaller board than the previous one, consisting of only six members. Three directors are partners from the private equity firm and there are two new external directors on the board. Plus an independent chairman. The CEO is not a board member but has been asked to present the results from the last reporting period. As the company was bought quite recently, the board meets every two months or upon request from either the CEO or the chairman.

One of the issues facing the company prior to the investment was the relatively poor profitability of the company. One of the first priorities of the new owner has thus been to focus on profit enhancement by implementing a comprehensive program to improve performance through cost-level reductions, productivity improvements, pricing strategy modification and the overhaul of the entire product range.

The CEO had been given this task two months earlier and he is now reporting back to the board for the first time. He brought his Executive VP sales and marketing with him, and they all listened to the outcome of the performance enhancement program that the board had heard of at last month's meeting.

The CEO ended his summary presentation by pointing out that the first part of the program had already resulted in an improvement in profit margins. He announced, 'We managed to increase our return on sales from eight to twelve per cent last month. A great improvement!'

He looked around the board for their reaction. He was quite disappointed when one of the partners said, 'Twelve per cent! That is not even close to the best of your competitors. You must go back and try harder!'

Reluctantly, the CEO left the room and went back to his team in the office of the portfolio company. 'We must all find ways to improve our margins. Please go out to your departments and come back to me and show how we could improve our position with prices, costs and where we stand in relation to competition. Then come back to me in a fortnight and report!'

The management team met again some weeks later, even as the results of the actions already implemented had started to show. After two months, the CEO felt ready to call another meeting with the board. The following is what happened.

> 'Good morning. I want to let you know that our company has managed to increase our margins to a record level of fifteen per cent. Never in the history of our business have we ever been this high!' he said with pride in his voice.

'Fifteen per cent is not good enough', his chairman said after having looked around the table. 'Go back and return to us with a better result as soon as you can!' The CEO almost lost his nerve but did not comment. Two months later the Board met again.

'We have now succeeded to bring the profit margin to eighteen per cent', the CEO explained.

'This was as much as we could do. We hope you are happy with our results', he added.

The board discussed the report presented by the CEO and his team for a while. Then the chairman asked for silence before saying, 'No Tim, eighteen per cent is not good enough. We know you are upset by this reply, and we owe you an explanation. But at the board we have looked very deep into your numbers and checked and compared with your competitors and best practice in other industries. What you have done is not bad at all, and you and the team have done a great job so far. But we have looked at the underlying drivers of your margins, and found that by making three additional improvements you should be able to be at twenty per cent margin.'

He added:

> First, you should increase prices in the high end of your range by an additional ten to fifteen per cent; then your distribution costs are at least ten per cent too high as they are more than five per cent higher the our competitors with roughly the same revenue levels. Finally, we believe that by investing in an overhaul of our IT systems, we should be able to improve our customer retention rate by a factor of 25%; from existing churn rate of 10% to 7.5%. We have calculated the positive EBIT impact to be somewhere around one per cent.

At first, the CEO was silent. He reflected on the chairman's message and then he answered, 'You are right! We should have thought about the churn rate and retention programs a long time ago. And you are also right about our distribution strategy and choice of channels. Let me go back to my team and then implement these proposals and ideas.'

Six months later, the CEO reported back to the last board meeting for the year. 'We are now at twenty per cent profit margin. You were right and we are happy for this!'

Lessons to be learned

Reality case: 'The Private Equity Portfolio Company Board'

- The board should push for superior performance.
- Good can always be done better!
- Performance focus is important but must be built on solid knowledge and insight about the key value drivers in the business.

Chapter 10
Setting strategic agendas

Setting the agenda

When analysing what a board spends most of its active time doing, at least during and in direct relation to the board meetings, it seems that their deliberations and decisions are very much driven by what is put on the agenda for the meeting. When probed about the agenda writing, one chairman admitted, 'My CEO's secretary is copying the headings of the last meeting; on very rare occasions have I or my CEO changed or added/removed an existing agenda item.'

A chairman of an oil exploration group shared this view with me:

> The only new intellectual contribution to what the board will be asked to deal with at the upcoming meeting, is what I and the CEO include under the last agenda point 'Other Items'; this is scary but unfortunately the reality in our company.

To add to this dire picture of board focus, this statement from a chairman of a bank:

> When we finally get to the last agenda item, the 'Other Issues' one, many board members start looking at their watches, and ask me if their taxi to the airport is on its way as agreed; as a result, we sometimes do not have enough time to discuss these unique decision or information points; it is a shame.

Now, if this is a common feature of most board's *modus operandi*, how could we then expect any board to devote enough time to strategy and strategic decision-making? Are all boards the prisoners of their own agenda? And, is this agenda in its turn really 'cast in iron'?

The board and strategy

In the research, with few exceptions, board members as well as CEOs were of the opinion that the board should be used to create value by getting more involved in key issues related to strategy. At the same time, it was clear that the actual execution of strategy should be left to the management team to carry out. As the following sections share, there are leveraged roles for the board to play in strategy implementation as well.

Most of the board members I interviewed agreed that the board should be involved in reviewing strategy on an ongoing basis. In fact, this is frequently set out as a key duty of the board by regulators. However, it is also important that they should also engage in the goal formulation process, thus getting directly involved in the strategy formulation process. Strategic goals cannot be defined and formulated unless the underlying strategy has been defined and vetted by the board.

By engaging in strategic goal formulation, the board is also bound to take part in the follow-up of goal accomplishment. This leads into performance evaluation and the issue of rewards and remuneration.

In order to achieve a functioning goal formulation and follow-up process, the board must spend adequate time on securing strategic alignment of the management team with the goals jointly defined and agreed upon. This implies a dedicated effort on behalf of the board and the chairman should take a lead role in this process as discussed in Chapter 6. Not everybody agreed to this strategic agenda and imperatives, however.

The chairman of a large financial services group gave this interesting view on the potential strategic role of the board:

> Board and strategy? No, that is clearly the wrong role for the board. Strategy is just a buzzword that is being used by consultants. Let them [the consultants] spend their time on such things instead of the board.

The chairman previously quoted was quite alone in this rather extreme view on the board and strategy. But similar views were sometimes expressed by others too, but more in the context of adding unwanted exposure to personal liability for board members, should their actions be challenged by shareholders or regulators. The sense of 'What is in it for me?' [to get actively involved in strategic company matters], was expressed by alarmingly high number of chairmen and senior board members during the interviews.

What could the board aspire to achieve from defining and setting the strategic agenda for its meetings? Or what strategic issues should the board engage in and what areas should be left outside of the board's involvement?

Board role in strategy formulation

Most companies have a strategy more or less clearly defined and articulated. Even the majority of young start-up businesses have an idea about what they should do and (hopefully) how to do it. However, it is a key task for the board to constantly monitor and review if the strategic direction of the corporation is still relevant.

A part of this role is to translate a strategy into defined and achievable strategic goals. That would lead the company down the desired strategic route to market and profitability. This goal formulation and follow-up process is a key task for the board. Given that the external factors impacting strategy are changing, and that new and unexpected events could force the corporation to rethink and alter its plans, the board must design a process whereby it can review and, if needed, rejuvenate the strategy of the business.

During the interviews for this book, a few very good examples of where a board had closely monitored the impact on the ongoing structural change in its industry were noted. Typically these led to consolidation and the build up of larger merged entities, and the parallel development of niche-oriented strategies. Similar examples of strategy reconsideration were found in the telecom sector. Here, technology change has forced both operators and vendors to rethink their traditional business models and strategies for profitable growth.

One interesting example from a board member in the fine chemicals industry illustrates this:

> We at the board concluded some time ago, that our company, that was a successful medium sized player in our industry, was facing a period of rapid industry consolidation and structural change. Larger groups were being formed through the purchase of smaller players, and through outright merger between equals. Simultaneously, smaller companies turned more and more to a pure niche oriented strategy, specializing in specific materials and applications. We were at risk of being 'stuck-in-the-middle'. So the board commissioned a strategy consultant to analyze the options available to us; they returned with two clear options, one to merge with a large company, the other to go down a route of acquiring smaller established niche companies. The board took ample time to consider the analysis and options presented by the consultants. We arranged a retreat for the board members over a weekend. No-one else was informed except the CEO, however not of the details of the task. We made it clear that this was a board issue, and that the rest of the management group was not to get involved or even be kept informed about the course of events and decisions. We came to the conclusion that we should go for the merger alternative and had also

identified our preferred merger partner. I was assigned the task of approaching the chairman of the larger group.

When asked about the rationale for keeping the process entirely at board level, and not involving management, the board member continued:

> We were a publicly traded stock corporation, and any increase in our stock price or that of our future partner to be, could have killed the whole plan. This was the main reason for this decision – but also the fact that I knew the chairman of the larger group.

He continued:

> I called the chairman of the merger candidate; he was very enthusiastic about the idea, and we met the following week. The two boards were kept informed all the time, and so were the two CEO's, but it was he and I who negotiated the entire deal structure including the terms and conditions of the deal. We had two face-to-face meetings with our board during the time it took to sign the deal. Upon signing we immediately informed the management teams and the rest of the organizations. I accepted a new role as a board member of the merged entity. My counterpart became the new chairman, a perfect solution for both of us.

One key issue related to this case of active board involvement, is to what extent the conclusion that the strategy needed to be rethought was the result of a systematic approach to strategy reviews and evaluation of strategic performance, or if it was more *ad hoc* and dictated by the events occurring around the company. In this particular case, the board spent one full day per year to review the strategic development of the business. It could be argued that the impetus to act was derived directly from such an ongoing strategy process. Another aspect of strategy formulation is the strategic goal formulation process. Typically, most corporations have established a set of performance goals, often linked to financial performance. To translate such goals into relevant and implementable actions, they should be defined as strategic and hence direct the long-term development of the business.

When asked about what strategic goals they used, if any, to guide their corporations, most board members mentioned 'growth' and 'market share' as the predominant objectives. Some added other parameters, such as 'rate of innovation' and 'key customer acquisition targets'. In fact, one major consumer services company CEO mentioned that the key strategic goal used in his company was 'customer retention' and 'loyalty/satisfaction goals'. He concluded:

> In our business, the ability to retain customers and add the 'share-of-wallet' for these customers is the key driver of value. Growth and market share is also relevant, but subordinated to the customer related goals. It works, and we are constantly monitoring these results and it is a key reporting item at our board meetings.

There were other similar examples of a functioning goal formulation and evaluation process. But the key point for the purpose of drawing conclusions from the research, is what boards actually could do to engage in the strategic goal formulation and follow-up process. The following are the findings in summary:

- The board should support management in defining and articulating relevant strategic goals. As is discussed in the preceding, one such goal used in a specific kind of business may not be appropriate in a different business and/or industry setting.
- A key task is to challenge strategic goals as being presented to it by executive management. Strategic goals typically reflect the chosen business model and existing strategy, and it would imply to remain with a strategic *status quo*, unless the board sees as its task to constantly challenge and critically review these goals and their underlying strategies.

- To challenge the strategic 'holy cows' and existing strategy paradigms are indeed key tasks for the board.
- The board should review and reconsider strategies, both at the dedicated strategy reviews which it should arrange on a regular basis, but could also undertake to carry out 'strategic audits' with regular intervals; sometimes this could involve engaging external resources such as strategy consultants to support the board and management in such reviews. Albeit sometimes expensive and resource demanding, it has shown in many cases to be a sound and effective investment in the future direction of the business.
- The board should follow-up and act on the strategic goal fulfilment of the executive management team; this could be done at dedicated strategy retreats.
- The board is also responsible for securing a close alignment between these goals and plans presented by management, not least regarding the performance evaluation and reward system.

All of this requires a carefully structured strategy process where the board is involved together with executive management as previously outlined.

Board role in strategy implementation

The prime responsibility for implementing strategy lies with executive management. However, certain tasks should involve the board if its members possess the relevant skills to add value to the strategic initiatives pursued by management.

As seen in the examples discussed, one such area is engaging in merger processes. In the specific case referred to, the boards and the chairmen were responsible for carrying out most of the key tasks involved in approaching, negotiating and closing the merger. This work also included planning for the future joint management structure of the merged entity, an aspect that effectively excludes the active involvement of the executives thus affected by such plans.

In more traditional acquisition projects, however, members of the board could be given an active role if they possess skills and core competencies that add value to the various parts of an acquisition initiative. The chairman could also be given a key role as lead negotiator, or just participate in a 'tandem' pair with the CEO. This latter approach has been mentioned by many senior board members as a very successful use of the board's resources.

The same applies to the involvement of individual board members in launching and negotiating major strategic partnerships as well as key customer agreements. In certain markets, it is a rule that the chairman and senior board members negotiate and close large commercial projects even without the involvement of the CEO and his C-level team. For example, this is true in many parts of Asia, where the chairman by tradition has a more prominent role than in Europe and other parts of the world.

A senior board member of a large pharmaceutical group told about his personal involvement to defend the corporation from a hostile takeover bid from a competitor:

> I had previous experience from having been under attack in my previous job as a CEO in another company; so our chairman asked me if I could step-up and coordinate the actions on our side with the goal of avoiding the acquisition to take place. We had analyzed the bidder and concluded that a sale would not be in the best interest of our shareholders. I worked almost full time with his process together with the CFO of the company. It was hard, but eventually we managed to fight them off. That saved lots of value for us. But I did not really have the time to do this, but when the chairman asked me, I could not say no; and everybody is happy that I did not.

Similar examples where board members and the chairman have been asked to take on a specific strategic task were given during the research. Several CEOs specifically told that they wanted to see the board becoming more active in supporting them and their management team in closing with large customers. Not only in typical project-based industries such as large telecom infrastructure sales, but also in investment banking, large distribution deals in the beverage industry and similar major strategic initiatives.

One CEO in a telecom company complained:

> My chairman has been leading this company for ten years now; five with me and five with my predecessor; he has not been to a single customer meeting since the day he took over the chair; and he knows this industry and the key players better than most. He has spent most of his active career in this space. Why is he not opening up doors for me and my team? I ask him but he seems to ignore the question. I have given up now.

Some conclusions can be drawn from this and the other situations encountered:

- The board members when engaging in certain specific strategic tasks where their background, skills and network could add value to the company represent a significant resource for the company.
- It is up to the chairman and the CEO to determine who and when a board member should be called in to support the executives; it must be done with a consensus between the CEO and the board member.
- If asked to engage in strategic tasks, the board member should expect to be rewarded accordingly; this is a delicate matter and must be negotiated in advance and be in line with the overall compensation policy of the corporation
- Typically, the chairman acts as the leader for such initiatives. Often, they are the resource required for the task themselves.

The board and use of strategy consultants

Strategy consultants offer valuable analytical skills and process experience to their clients. Many top tier firms also possess considerable industry expertise and have the ability to support the board when analysing the strategic context of the situation a company is in. Engaging external advisors must always be done with a clear view on what exactly they should be asked to do, and what the expected deliverables are. Open-ended and never-ending assignments have proven to be very negative for many companies. With the right brief and expectations, however, strategy consultants can add significant value in the strategy process.

There are other interesting examples of how companies try to enhance the strategic aspects of board work, by electing former senior strategy consultants to join their boards as directors. One well-known example is the board position that was held by Rajat Gupta, former Head of McKinsey & Company, at Goldman Sachs.

Recently, Gupta's former partner and once his contender for the top management position in McKinsey, Christian Caspar was elected to the Board of Industrivärden, a powerful Swedish holding company (with large holdings in Ericsson, Sandvik, Handelsbanken and other large Swedish multinationals).

There are other similar appointments that could be interpreted as a sign of desire to increase the strategic competence and experience at board level. Research to analyse to what extent such engagements of former strategy consultants at board level have resulted in any changes in the way those boards have approached and dealt with strategy is not yet available. The phenomenon is interesting, however, and could show that strategy is increasingly getting on to the board agenda.

This is not to say that boards have not been using strategy consultants extensively in the past. Bain & Company, for example, were often engaged by corporate boards to evaluate various strategic options and recommend the board and management on strategy implementation. Frequently, significant strategic change and value creation came out from the subsequent implementation of these recommendations to management.

Unfortunately, the use of external strategy consultants can also be used to create a 'rubber stamp' for board approval of actions that management has already vetted and agreed to implement. This is obviously a major flaw as well as waste of time and resources.

The board in action: the strategy retreat initiative

Many boards spend one meeting per year reviewing and discussing strategy. Unfortunately, many of the examples observed, were more of a mere information sharing nature, where the CEO asks the business line managers to present their respective businesses to the board, in endless slide presentations with huge data on the business, competition, prospects and, sometimes, strategic options for decision-making.

One chairman of a large food conglomerate said:

> When the CEO asked his business area managers to present their businesses for us, we were given what I call 'PowerPoint Waterfalls' where enormous amounts of data were presented without any real strategic issues defined, and no decision-making points or options put forward for consideration and even less for decision; a complete waste of time.

It is true, however, that this kind of exchange of views and analysis of the strategic performance of the business fulfils a key role in the overall strategy process.

If well prepared and focusing on relevant strategic issues and options for strategic development of the business, strategy retreats, especially when arranged offsite so as to avoid the interference of day-to-day work tasks, can offer the management and the board the opportunity to both review and impact the strategic direction of the company.

It also gives the board the opportunity to intervene if it finds that management has come to a point where the existing strategy and prevailing business model need rethinking.

One chairman of a design group observed:

> I spend lots of time preparing for our bi-annual two day strategy retreat, together with the CEO, but also with my advisors. We have a special 'Chairman's Committee' where the main task is to prepare these events twice per year. Sometimes we ask outside consultants to help us to develop relevant material and program content, but most of the time we do it together internally. These retreats are very likely the best elements of our entire strategy process.

The board and strategy: concluding remarks

To summarize, the board could and should play a key role in strategy formulation, goal formulation, strategy reviews and implementation of key strategic initiatives. This requires that the skills and competencies of the board members are all brought to bear on the key value drivers of the business. The chairman should lead this process together with the CEO. He/she should also complement the skill base and networks of the board members so as to enhance the value creation potential of the board. As one CEO put it in an interview:

> The board is a hidden treasure; they have so many great skills and contacts. I should ask them to work with me much more actively than we do at present. I just need to better know what they are specifically good at; here the chairman helps me a lot.

At all times, the distinction between the executive tasks of the management team and the potential support role of the board must be kept in mind and respected. Used in the right way, this 'hidden treasure' could create significant value for management and the shareholders.

Reality case

The Strategy consultants in the board room

An industrial group had experienced severe problems with its levels of profitability during the period following the financial crisis. At a crisis meeting between the chairman and the largest owners back in March of 2011, it was decided to replace the CEO. After having called an extraordinary shareholder meeting in May, it was also decided to substitute some of the former board members. The CEO had started with immediate effect in September. The new board has met for the first time in early July.

The board had reviewed the situation in the group together with the CEO and his management team for an entire weekend. The outcome was that a small group of the board members were appointed as responsible for reviewing the strategy of the group in a joint effort together with the CEO. It was decided to engage a strategy consulting firm to conduct the analysis of the portfolio of business units in the group, and to recommend the board a corporate strategy going forward. The CEO and the strategy review group engaged a well-known firm after a careful selection process and the consultants started their work in November. The partner in charge of the work reported to the strategy review group, not to the CEO alone. The strategy consultants started the work in September.

The first thing that took place was to establish a set of 'c' criteria for corporate strategy priorities. Such criteria were derived from the overall strategic and financial goals for the group. The underlying principle was that a business unit could be evaluated against these criteria and then be deemed to either fit or not in the future strategic scope of the group. These criteria were then embedded into the analytical work of the consultants.

Progress reports were presented every month. The duration of the first analytical phase was not to exceed two months. The second phase consisted in evaluating the business units against the set of corporate strategy criteria set forth by the strategy review group. It should be noted that a couple of the board members actually wanted to define and set the strategic criteria together with the consultants so that the strategy formulation dimension also became part of the assignment. But the chairman and the CEO jointly decided against such a solution. 'Strategy formulation should be the responsibility of the board', the chairman had said. 'We have already established long-term goals for the group, so we just have to translate those into the strategic criteria. This is the responsibility of the board', he added. This principle had been accepted by everybody.

At the end of the second phase, a preliminary recommendation for the future composition of the group was presented by the consultants and agreed upon by the strategy review group. It was decided that a third phase to be presented in February of the next year.

The third phase of the work that aimed at developing strategic plans for the proposed core business units aimed at understanding the resources required to reach their potential. This was an iterative process where the partner of the firm met with the strategy review group on a more frequent basis throughout the early spring.

Having concluded that the net cash flow implications of the proposed divestment and growth plans was in line with the financial position of the group, the entire board and the management team was asked to assemble for a strategy retreat at a site outside of the group's head office. The new strategy was discussed and approved together with the CEO and his

Setting strategic agendas

management team. Clear instructions for implementation were discussed and approved. The CEO was given the mandate to find buyers for the noncore businesses at prices to be discussed and agreed with the strategy review group and then approved by the board as a whole.

The chairman and the CEO were scheduled to meet every two weeks to monitor progress of the implementation process. The strategy consultants were thanked and their bill was paid. Although the managing partner volunteered to of part of the implementation work, the board politely said no.

'Strategy formulation is the responsibility of the board, and implementation of the strategic plan should be the responsibility of executive management', the chairman declared after the completion of the final presentation and summary discussion with the consultant team.

Lessons to be learned

Reality case: 'The Strategy Consultants in the Boardroom'

- A fundamental strategy review enables the board to challenge the existing strategy pursued by executive management.
- Both the board as well as executive management must commit to the initiative. They must be 'on the same page'.
- Purpose and deliverables must be carefully defined and review process limited in time and cost.
- Progress reports are imperative, and the final report should be made to both board and management.

CHAPTER 11
Summary and conclusions

A brief summary

When I set out to study the many complex issues related to the role of the board in a corporation, my hypothesis was (and remains) that a board should be given a role that is more focused on value creation and active involvement in the key strategic initiatives and core business processes of the company. The implicit assumption was that this would not be the case in many corporations, and that a great potential for improvement and change for the better exists.

However, one important factor I had to gain a better grasp of was whether this view was indeed shared with the people actively working at the board level today. I also wanted to get a better understanding of the leadership issues related to the *modus operandi* and role of the board. Thus, I chose to meet with and interview in depth a group of very distinguished chairmen and senior members of boards in corporations worldwide. I also met with a number of CEOs and owner representatives on boards. My underlying belief was that no such change is possible unless there is leadership in place to implement such initiatives. Also, that leadership must come from the board itself and through the chairman of the board, who is the board leader.

I have some experience from board work myself, both in listed and in privately owned companies, where I have been the chairman as well as a board director. I have also built relevant experience from having served in several CEO positions over the years. However, I wanted to find out the views and insights of the senior and experienced executives I met, without having any predetermined views on how things are, how things should be or how change could be accomplished.

My focus has been on the role the board could play in creating value for the corporation. By defining the most relevant and value-oriented role for the board that is possible, and by altering its way of acting, its *modus operandi* to be more efficient, the board should focus more on the right things. This should also be the case as well as for shareholders to aim at achieving a composition of the board that reflects diversity and a set of core competencies that would enhance its performance and contribute to value creation for the corporation.

I am aware that there are large cultural and regulatory differences involved that affect the way the board works. These differences also put limitations on what kind of changes that could *de facto* be carried out if change should be called for or wanted. However, I also believe that a board could become truly valued and creation focused, if it really wants to, by asking itself, 'What could we do to create value for this company?'

All Above Board: ten lessons taught

Lesson number one: 'change is possible'

With almost no exceptions, the chairmen and senior executives I met and interviewed were firmly of the opinion that the board could add more value to the corporation, and that the change required to enhance the value creation potential of the board was possible.

Lesson number two: 'the board is appointed by the owner to represent his/her interest'

A board member is appointed to serve the interests of the owner, and the board must understand and implement the vision as well as the long-term goals of the owner. To be a board member does not mean having been given a tool and a playing field for your own use. The members must act and dedicate time in the interests of the owner, not for management or for oneself. Never forget this core pillar of our governance structure and principles.

Next, the board can play an active role in both strategy formulation and implementation. They can act both as a group of directors as well as through individual board members to support management in key strategic tasks, such as developing key customer accounts, generating and supporting in M&A deals and so on.

Lesson number three: 'the board should take an active role in strategy'

A key imperative for strategic development of the business is its ability to constantly drive new ideas and concepts, to push for innovation. By innovation, we should not only look at investments in R&D, but in new design, business models, concepts and disruptive strategies beyond pure technology development. Here the board should play an active role by constantly promoting and rewarding innovation and innovative behaviour.

Every business is exposed to the changes that take place in its external environment. The most prominent of these changes is the occurrence of business cycles.

Lesson number four: 'the board should act as a guide and leader for the corporation in times of change and disruption'

Organizations tend to foster many values and beliefs that could be based on resistance to change and innovation. We find many cases where such 'Holy Cows' and paradigms could turn out to be disastrous for the company in the long term. The board must challenge such unwillingness to change and at the same time act as a catalyst for change and new ideas.

Lesson number five: 'the board should push for innovation'

A board is a group of individuals who each contributes based on his/her skills and core competence. This should be leveraged so as to use the best man/woman in each role. However, the real strength of the board is when it acts as a team, when cross-fertilization between board members are used to its full potential.

Therefore, the board should be composed of members whose individual skills and competencies are complementary and aligned with the nature and scope of the business of the corporation. Diversity could bring lots of value to the performance potential of the board.

Lesson number six: 'the board members should be recruited to match the specific needs of the corporation'

The board should also act as a group where 'synergies' between the individual members add to the combined full potential of the board for value creation for the corporation. Thus, the goal is to achieve those synergies through bringing the combined skills of the board members to bear.

Lesson number seven: 'the board should act as one team'

Each team needs a leader and a coach. The chosen and elected leader of the board is its chairman. In the research, I met with and interviewed many chairmen and their combined experiences form the basis for most of my conclusions and recommendations. However, the role of the chairman must be further enhanced and leveraged. The chairman him-/herself must be the right leader for the board and corporation.

Lesson number eight: 'the chairman should be a strong leader for the board and his/her selection should be based on superior competence'

The chairman is not the executive leader of the corporation; this is the role of the CEO. Successful companies have established a strong partnership between the two top leaders. Such a partnership is built on mutual respect and an agreed division of roles and responsibilities between them. A 'win-win' relationship between the chairman and the CEO is a must for a company if it aspires to become excellent.

Lesson number nine: 'create a tandem duo at the top'

Too much of the board's time and effort is spent on pure control and governance issues. Albeit important and certainly a key task of the board, a common theme amongst the chairmen I interviewed was that the board should focus on how to improve the performance of the corporation as a whole. Successful boards do so by being knowledgeable and insightful about the underlying business of the corporation, and by constantly probing the management team to improve its performance levels.

Lesson number ten: 'boost peak performance of the corporation'

To summarize, throughout the research, almost every single chairman I met emphasized the imperative for a better use and simultaneous improvement of the skills and competencies of the board. This requires a change in the roles and key tasks of the board as compared with what most boards do today. Some companies have succeeded in capturing the power of a strong and competent board. It is shown in the underlying strategic and operating performance of the company. Therefore, the final lesson is the sum total of the previous ten, a lesson to be learned from *All Above Board – the board should use its full potential to create value for the corporation.*

CHAPTER 12
Research methodology

Background to the research initiative for *All Above Board*[1]

I have always been interested in the areas of strategy and leadership, as these are implemented in both entrepreneurial organizations and in large complex corporations. Both in my academic work as adjunct professor of Entrepreneurship at INSEAD and also as visiting professor of Entrepreneurship at the Stockholm School of Entrepreneurship, the role and influence of leaders on strategy and thus on value creation in the business, have always been themes of keen interest to me. In my professional career both as senior partner of Bain & Company, and as advisor and manager in the private equity industry, the focus on leadership and strategy has been a key issue. Finally, as chairman and board member of several companies, both small and large, I have been exposed to the set of critical issues that a board faces. I have also seen how often the board is either ignored or is not used in a way that it be should in order to leverage its potential to create value for the corporation it serves.

Such leadership issues are not limited to the management team, however. The board plays a key role in the overall strategic direction and leadership of the company, albeit many times forgotten or ignored, or is involved in governance issues only. When I worked together with Peter Lorange at the Lorange Institute of Business, we found that we both shared a keen interest in the role of the board and how this could be improved so as to allow the board to add value, and to avoid

Research methodology

the myriad of pitfalls that we both had observed as academics analysing issues related to strategy and leadership, and as active business people with significant management and board membership experience of our own.

We decided to launch this research initiative together. Initially, we both worked on the analytical phase conducting interviews and meeting with board members and chairmen. Over time, it became natural that I continued with the research work alone. Therefore, the results and findings from the research are mostly my own. However, I wish to extend a deep gratitude to Peter Lorange for his support and also for having contributed to define and develop the conceptual framework for this research initiative and for its key findings.

Scope of the research

The initial research for *All Above Board* was designed based on intensive studies of prevailing literature on the subjects related to the role of the Board of Directors. It is interesting to note that, since the early work presented by Peter Drucker in *The Practice of Management* (1955), very little has been written and researched on the roles performed by and assigned to the board in corporations. Even less has been written on the sole subject of the role of the chairman in corporations. Of course, some interesting research has been carried out since the time of Drucker's book. Most of this research has focused on governance and regulatory issues associated with boards. Recently, the topic of diversity, especially gender diversity has been the focus of scientific interest.

Surprisingly, little has been done in the area of specific concern for my own research. That is on issues related to the potential for the board to create value for the corporation it serves, and how this value creation role is affected by the very nature of board work, that is, its focus, as well as its composition and *modus operandi*. This, including the leadership role of the chairman and how he/she partners with the CEO in a tandem leadership role, is what I set out to study. The underlying paradigm for my research is that boards could and should perform strategic roles and leadership and use a *modus operandi* to create value for the corporation.

There are some good reasons for this lack of research focus on issues related to strategy and leadership. One is the confidential nature of board matters and decision making. Others are the difficulty of getting access to the chairmen and top level board members and the reluctance some board members seem to have to discuss their board engagements. Finally, the minutes from board meetings are many times highly sensitive in their content, and by definition 'classified' and confidential in nature. Not even the chairman could give authorization for researchers to have access to such files.

Target sample and selection

I have met with a total of 48 chairmen of the board in larger corporations, all in all representing over 532 board chair positions. In addition, we have discussed key board-related issues with another 20 board members of large multinationals where we have had previous relationships and on-going discussions. Finally, I met with over 50 CEOs. Interviews were open-ended but we focused the discussions on three core themes.

Potential targets for interviews were selected in the following ways:

1. A selection was made of half the corporations from the Fortune 500 2009 List. The response rate was ca. 10 per cent, that is, 26 chairmen accepted to participate in the study out of the 250 approached by us.
2. A selection of an additional 22 chairmen where the researcher had an existing personal contact with the chairman and/or CEO.

3. In some cases, the interviewee was not the chairman but another senior board member of the corporation; in no case was a board member and the chairman of the same corporation selected for an interview. In total, 22 additional board members were interviewed. If the board members of these corporations are added, the response rate from the Fortune 500 sample raises to 15 per cent.
4. Fifteen of the chairmen and board members were serving on more than one corporation's board. One chairman served on a total of six boards.
5. In addition, 30 CEOs in the same and other corporations were also selected for interviews. 10 of the CEOs were working in the same corporation as the chairmen interviewed. Three CEOs were also the chairman of the company.

The breakdown of the interview sample is shown in the following breakdown.

Total number of Executives	Interviewed
Chairman of the board	48
Senior board Member	22
CEO	50

Corporations, total 120.

The sample is biased towards European-based corporations. This is partly due to the nature of existing relationships and the researcher's proprietary contact network. Another reason for the geographical bias is the lack of a sufficiently large budget for the research initiative. This constraint limited the amount of travel and prohibited extensive interview rounds such as in Asia and Latin America. Partly, this was handled through the telephone and Skype interviews. It is important to bear this limitation of the interview targets in mind when analysing both the findings and the conclusions and recommendations based therein.

The geographical breakdown of corporations is shown in the following.

Region/Country	No. of corporations	% of total
Europe	76	63%
North America	21	18%
Latin America	2	2%
Asia	12	10%
Middle East	5	4%
Rest of World	4	3%
Total	120	100%

The main focus for the research has been on the role of the board in large corporations. I am fully aware that the board plays a significant role in all stages of the development of a company, not least in many start-up businesses where I have personally spent a lot of time working.

But given the complexity of managing large organizations, it was decided to focus this study on a selection of corporations listed on the Fortune 500 List for 2009. The distribution of size of the companies in the research is shown here:

Revenues* (USD millions)	% of corporations
>10 000	33
5–10 000	40
1–5 000	14
<1000	13

Note: *For banks, the figure was for total assets.

Interview preparation and conduct

The broad themes outlined in the following were presented in a letter to the chairmen sent out prior to the interviews:

1. The actual tasks performed by the board, around what was called the 'agenda'.

2. The relationship between the board including the chairman and the owner/-s.
3. The effectiveness of board decision making and the composition of the board ('the team' and the 'committees').
4. The strategic role of the board in innovation, strategy formulation and implementation, and performance enhancement.

At each interview, handwritten notes were taken and in some cases later shared with the interviewee.

Some interviews were carried out by telephone or via Skype, mainly due to time and cost considerations. Most interviews lasted between one and two hours. With some exceptions, the discussions continued for over three to four hours.

In two cases, the chairman insisted on continuing the discussions together with the entire board. This was done in separate offsite meetings where the discussions about the role of the board and its *modus operandi* were being held in conjunction with a regular board meeting. These discussions, as well as other separately arranged board seminars, gave me the chance to test my findings and helped me to refine the conclusions and recommendations presented in this book.

At three other interview occasions, the chairman brought the CEO along to the meeting and interview/discussion. This was not preferred, but was accepted nevertheless.

Notes

Chapter 2 The board of the future

This chapter is written by Ulf Lindgren with Peter Lorange. Peter Lorange is a Norwegian academic known for his pioneering work on issues related to corporate strategy and organization. He is President and owner of the Lorange Institute of Business Zürich, He has previously been President of IMD and President of the Norwegian School of Management. He has taught at the Wharton School, University of Pennsylvania and at the MIT Sloan School of Management, Norwegian School of Business (BI), IMD and now at the Lorange Institute of Business.

1. A story told by a Vice Chairman of a Scandinavian Industrial Group.

Chapter 12 Research methodology

1. The name of the original research initiative is *The Board of the Future*.
2. Five chairmen chaired two boards.

Index

absent owners, 64
active ownership, 45–6, 47–9
Advisory Board, 100–3, 106–7
agenda, 8–9
   setting strategic, 141–55
   for shareholder meetings, 62–4
AGM, 63–4
Ambra project, 116–17
Amelio, Gil, 3
annual meetings, 63
Apple, 2–5

Bain & Company, 41–2, 150–1
Basel III rules, 38
Bebchuk, Lucian, 64
benchmarking, 124
Black Swans, 97–9
board bypassing, 50, 61
board instructions, 41
board meetings
  agenda-setting for, 8–9
  example, 14–17
board of directors
  Black Swans and, 97–9
  business cycles and, 92–7, 104
  composition of, 6
  design of optimal, 7–8
  election of, by shareholders, 41
  as hidden asset, 6–7
  hijacking of, 71, 77–8, 81
  Holy Cows and, 99–100
  innovation and, 110–22, 158–9
  interaction between CEO and, 34
  interaction between chairman and, 34
  interaction between owner and, 49–59
  lack of key skills and competencies on, 78
  leadership in times of change and disruption, 85–109, 158–9
  'one team' board, 69–84, 150–60
  optimal, 69–70
  overly large, 79–80
  owner and, 40–68
  owner's interests and, 157–8
  performance-based culture and, 125–8
  performance of, 6–7
  power struggles at level of, 73–4
  recruitment of, 158–9
  role of, 1, 23–4, 156–7
  strategic agenda setting by, 141–55, 158
  structure of, 18
  value creating, 110–22
  visible, 64–5
  women on, 79–80, 81–2
board-on-the-board, 60
board strategy retreats, 22–3
BP, 99
bubbles, 90–2
business cycles, 90, 92–7, 104, 107–9
business models
  developing new, 11–12, 88
  separate, 116–17

Campbell, Bill, 4
capital market interaction, 33

169

Index

chairman, 1
  challenges and opportunities for, 22–4
  combined with CEO role, 36
  emergence of new role for, 24–5
  enhancing value of, 18–28
  interaction with board, 34
  interaction with owner, 50–1, 60
  key executive tasks for, 22
  lack of leadership by, 76–7
  leadership by, 81, 160
  new, 25–8
  relationship between CEO and, 7–8, 29–39
  role of, 18–24, 150–60
  as spokesman of corporation, 23
Chairman Committee, 9, 53–5, 152
change, 157
  board as catalyst for, 87–9, 103
  in external environment, 92–7
  proactive, 88
  reacting to, 89–92
  resistance to, 87–9, 158–9
change leadership, 85–109, 158–9
Chief Executive Officer (CEO), 1
  combined with chairman role, 36
  interaction with board, 34
  quarterly report to owners by, 58–9
  relationship between chairman and, 7–8, 29–39
codes of conduct, 41
committees, 9–10, 32
common values, 70
common vision/goals, lack of, 72
Compensation Committee, 9, 32, 37–8
compensation structure, 37–8
corporate governance, 41, 50
  board and owner interaction, 49–66
  rules for, 41, 62–3

corporate laws, 41
corporate strategy, owner's vision and, 47–9, 61–2
corporate venture capital arms, 117–18
credit default swaps, 90
crisis management, 33, 97–9, 104–5
culture, performance-based, 12–13, 125–8, 135–7
customer acquisition, 33
customer needs, 10–11, 114
cycles, 92–7, 104, 107–9

Diamond, Jared, 91
diversity
  encouraging, 81–2
  gender, 78–80, 81–2
  lack of, 71, 78–9
dotcom crash, 91
Drucker, Peter, 18, 29, 30, 35, 93, 111, 163

Easter Island, 91, 99
economic cycles, 90, 92–7, 104, 107–9
elite clique, 60
Ellison, Larry, 4
EQT, 52–3
Experience Bank, 100–3, 106–7

family-owned enterprises, 41, 47, 61, 74, 76
financial crisis, 44, 90
first mover advantages, 88
Folksam Group, 67
forecasting models, 95
foreign subsidiaries, 46
founder, role of, 45
France, 55–6
free float, 62

'gap' creation, 12–13
gender diversity, 78–82

Index

Germany, corporate governance procedures in, 62–3
Ghang, Gareth, 4
goals
  lack of common, 72
  performance, 146
  strategic, 141–55
goal setting, 95–6, 134–5
Gore, Al, 4
governance structures, 52–8
governor role, 20
Gupta, Rajat, 150

Hasselgren, Raoul, 119–20, 121
hedge funds, 23–4, 43
hijacking of board, 71, 77–8, 81
Holy Cows, 99–100, 105–6, 110, 111, 147, 158–9
housing bubble, 91–2

IBM, 116–17
incentive systems, 126–7, 134–5
information gathering, 130–1
information sharing, 33–4
in-house laboratories, 117
innovation, 10–11, 87, 88
  board of directors and, 110–22, 158–9
  board perspective on, 112–13
  business-oriented view of, 111–12
  resources for, 115
  rewarding, 115
  value creation through, 110–22
insightful board, 129–31, 137
institutional ownership, 40, 43–4, 49–50
Intel Capital, 117
intrapreneurship initiatives, 118
investment managers, 44, 49
Isacsson, Walter, 2

Jobs, Steve, 2–5

law of performance, 123–5
leadership, 1, 45
  by chairman, 81, 160
  in crisis, 104–5
  lack of, 76–7
  tandem, 30–9
  in times of change and disruption, 85–109
Leadership Premium, 106–7
Lehman Brothers, 91, 128
Leksell, Laurent, 46
Levinson, Art, 4
Lewis, Michael, 90
Lorange, Peter, 162–3
Lundin, Adolf, 66
Lundin, Ian, 68
Lundin Petroleum (LP), 66–8

Magnusson, Bernt, 120
Markides, Constantinos, 111–12, 116
Maya culture, 91
McKinsey & Company, 150
member selection, 7
mergers and acquisitions (M&A), 32–3, 119
mismanagement, 44
mission statement, 63
Modus Vivendi, for board and owner interaction, 49–66

Nespresso, 116
NK, 119–22
Nokia Ventures, 117
Nominating Committee, 9, 32, 70–1, 75–6, 78, 81

old boys network, 7, 30, 32, 78, 81
'one team' board, 69–84, 150–60
outliers, 97–9
ownerless corporations, 49–50
owner liaison director, 55–6, 64

owner liaison officer, 64–5
owner/ownership
  absent, 64
  active, 47–9
  aligning, 62–4
  board of directors and, 40–68
  CEO quarterly report to, 58–9
  family-owned enterprises, 41, 47, 61
  institutional, 40, 43–4, 49–50
  interaction between board and, 49–59
  interaction with chairman, 50–1, 60
  lack of direct, 42–5, 49–50
  private, 42–3
  private equity, 43, 46
  rejuvenating role of, 65–6
  state-owned enterprises, 42
  translation of vision of, into corporate strategy, 47–9, 61–2
  virtues of active, 45–6
  visible, 64–5
owner representative, 44, 49, 58, 70
owners' forum, 56–8

paradigm
  challenging reigning, 11–12, 105–6, 158–9
  changing the, 99–100
past, learning from the, 89–92
Paulson, Hank, 90
peak performance
  boosting, 123–40, 160–1
  culture of, 135–7
performance
  boosting peak, 123–40, 160–1
  law of, 123–5
  pursuit of superior, 137–40
  reward systems, 134–5
  reward systems for, 126–7
  roadmap, 132–3, 136

  targets, 124, 126–7, 146
  underperformance, 124, 126
  value creation through boosting, 128–37
performance-based culture, 12–13, 125–8, 135–7
performance management, 88
power struggles, 73–4
President Director General (PDG), 55–6
Presidium, 52, 60
private equity firms, 124–5
private equity ownership, 43, 46, 79
private owners, 42–3
proactive change, 88

quarterly report to owners, 58–9
quotas, 80, 82

recessions, 90
research and development (R&D), 10–11, 110, 111, 115, 119
research methodology, 162–7
reward systems, 126–7, 134–5
Risk Committee, 9, 98
roadmap technique, 132–3, 136

Sachs, Josef, 120
satisfactory underperformance, 124, 126
Schmidt, Eric, 4
senior advisors, 100–3, 106–7
Separation Strategy, 116–17
shareholder meetings, 41, 51, 62–4
shareholders, 6
  board of directors and, 40–68
  election of board by, 41
  small, 62–3
Shareholders Rights Project, 64
Sorkin, Andrew Ross, 90
speculative bubbles, 90–1
state-owned enterprises, 42

Index

status quo
   challenging, 11–12, 86–7
   strategic, 146
strategic agenda, 141–55, 158
strategic change, 86–7
strategic direction, 1, 8–9, 61–2, 63–4
strategic opportunities, 33
strategic vision, 126
strategy committee, 60
strategy consultants, 150–1, 153–5
strategy implementation, 147–9
strategy retreats, 72, 151–2
sub-committees, 9–10
subprime mortgage crisis, 91–2
subsidiaries, 46
succession procedures, 34

Takeda Group, 101
Taleb, Nassem, 97–8
tandem role, 21, 24
tandem structure, 19, 24, 29–39, 160
target setting, 95–6
team building experiences, 82–4
team leader, 20
team players, 8
teamwork, 22–3
Telia, 118
Telia Business Innovation, 118
termination procedures, 34

top leader role, 19–20
transparency, 63
TROIKA, 52–3, 60
true potential, 131–2
Tulip mania, 91

unexpected situations, 97–9
United States, corporate governance procedures in, 62, 63
unknown situations, 97–9

value creation, 23–4, 45, 46
   through innovation, 110–22
   through systematic approach to boosting performance, 128–37
value creator, 20–1
value statement, 63
Vandermerwe, Sandra, 118–19
visible boards, 64–5
visible owners, 64–5

women, as board members, 79–80, 81–2
Woolard, Ed, 3, 4
world-class companies, 12–13

York, Jerry, 4

Zuckerman, Gregory, 90

Printed and bound by CPI Group (UK) Ltd, Croydon, CR0 4YY